West Shore Country Club

A PICTORIAL HISTORY

West Shore Country Club

A PICTORIAL HISTORY

THE
DONNING COMPANY
PUBLISHERS

The Donning Company Publishers
184 Business Park Drive, Suite 206
Virginia Beach, VA 23462

Steve Mull, *General Manager*
Barbara Buchanan, *Office Manager*
Heather L. Floyd, *Editor*
Stephanie Danko, *Graphic Designer*
Derek Eley, *Imaging Artist*
Susan Adams, *Project Research Coordinator*
Tonya Hannink, *Marketing Specialist*
Pamela Engelhard, *Marketing Advisor*

Mary Taylor-Miller, Project Director

Library of Congress Cataloging-in-Publication Data

Latham, Robert, 1957-
  West Shore Country Club : a pictorial history / by Robert Latham.
     p. cm.
  ISBN 978-1-57864-593-0 (hbk. : alk. paper)
  1. West Shore Country Club (Camp Hill, Pa.)—History. 2. Country clubs—Pennsylvania—History. 3. Golf courses—Pennsylvania—History. I. Title.
  HS2725.C22W445 2009
  367'.974843—dc22
                                                            2009047617

Printed in the United States of America at Walsworth Publishing Company

Contents

Acknowledgments

Having a keen interest in history, 2006 Club president Bill Greenlee suggested we consider authorizing a book compiling the history of West Shore Country Club from its beginnings to the present. General Manager Scott Irwin had become aware of Donning Company Publishers through his attendance at annual meetings of the country club managers' association. That year, the Board of Governors authorized the financing of this publication and work began in earnest.

A wonderful, hardworking committee comprised of Bill Greenlee (past president), Scott Irwin, Dr. Alex McKechnie, Donna Saxon, Ray Gover, Bob Hetherington, Nellie Swarts (past president), Tim MacLean, Dawn Gribb, and I began soliciting information, photos, etc. and the book began to come together.

We sincerely appreciate the outpouring of information and contributions of many Club members. Shared memories, photographs, and memorabilia began to fall into place.

Particularly, we appreciate the contributions of Jeff Gribb, who authored the section on the golf course. We also thank Jim Tabor for sharing his family photos and for his help in developing the sections on his father, Ed Tabor, and the hole-by-hole tour of the golf course. The 2008 president Henry Line gave his support financially by backing a request to fund the services of Gale Varney, our editor. He also pressed hard for good information on the roots of the golf course from Old Tom Morris. Dawn Gribb, whose Gribb Graphics produces WSCC's monthly *Drumbeat*, provided most, if not all, of the more recent photos of the golf course and activities.

We thank Karen Paris of Hospice of Central PA for all of her help in authoring the section on West Shore's involvement with that great organization.

We acknowledge the contribution by *Harrisburg Magazine* for their permission to reprint "Golfer Prevails Over Handicap," authored by Scott Campbell and published October 2007 in the magazine.

Special thanks to Ray Gover and to the *Patriot News*, as Ray requested and the *Patriot* graciously provided photos from its archives.

Gail Varney's creative and editorial advice was crucial to the success of the book.

Finally, we appreciate all of the support from the great staff at West Shore Country Club in helping with photo storage, meeting arrangements, and copies, and especially Valerie Dolan, for retyping Dr. Alex's notes.

Robert E. Latham
June 2009

Foreword

In 1928, Franklin Davies gathered some friends together to form our great Club. Winds of uncertainty were blowing at the time. Throughout the following eighty years, the Club has grown in membership and in stature into what can be called, without boast, the premier country club in the Harrisburg area.

Since our Club's beginnings, we have seen world war, space travel, instant communication, and vast advances in technology. The golf game has changed from hickory shafts to titanium heads with literally hundreds of choices in club shafts. And tennis players of the past would hardly recognize the game and its equipment today.

The book you are about to enjoy is a celebration of the spirit of our members past and present and the camaraderie of this special place that originated from a farm adjacent to a one-room schoolhouse. We started with a modest clubhouse and three holes of golf. Won't you turn the pages of this book and enjoy the journey that has led us where we are today?

Gregg R. Aversa
President

1

ORIGINS OF
WEST SHORE COUNTRY CLUB LAND

The Delaware and Shawanese Indians inhabited the Cumberland Valley when the white man first arrived. The first battle between these two tribes took place between the squaws when they quarreled over the possession of a grasshopper found by one of the children. The warriors of both sides then engaged in a bloody battle and the defeated Shawanese moved west to the banks of the Ohio.

In about 1731, John Wright, Tobias Hendricks, and Samuel Blunston laid out the tracts of land on both sides of the Susquehanna and designated areas for the exclusive use of Indians. In early deeds, this area was named the Manor of Paxtang, or, sometimes, the Manor of the Conodoguinet. Eventually, it was named the Manor of Lowther, after an English gentleman who was married to William Penn's sister.

The ferry on the east side of the river was known as *Harris's Ferry*, and on the West Shore, it was called *Kelso's Ferry* after William Kelso, who lived in an old stone house built in 1734. He operated the ferry, valued at $3,500 in the East Pennsboro tax list, from 1769 until 1807. John Wormley also operated a ferry located in what is now Wormleysburg, valued at $500 on the tax list in 1793. Both ferries ceased to exist when a bridge was completed across the river.

There were two roads from the Susquehanna River to Carlisle. The "Great Road" was the main route, but near Tobias Hendricks's place, another road diverged from it, passing by the Trindle Spring. It became known as Trindle Spring Road. However, the road was not legally authorized by decree of the court, so as settlers began to fence in their properties, the road was fenced out of its direct course. People along this road actively petitioned the government for over twenty years to make the Trindle Spring Road a turnpike, but the "Great Road" (now the Carlisle Pike) eventually won that designation.

The Hendricks family name is inseparably connected with this locality. In fact, a Thomas A. Hendricks was a vice president of the United States. The home of Tobias Hendricks was in the Manor of Lowther. A Captain William Hendricks in 1775 led a company of ninety men from Carlisle to Boston to join Washington's army. They were assigned to Colonel Benedict Arnold's command in the invasion of Canada's Quebec.

In the 1730s, a Tobias Hendricks settled on the reservation to see that the Indians were not disturbed in their possession of this land on the west bank of the Susquehanna River. He was one of the

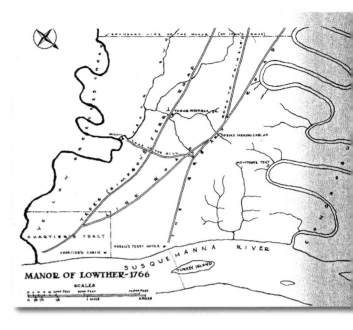

Manor of Lowther, 1766. Future site of West Shore Country Club located on the tract of Tobias Hendricks, Jr.

first to be a justice of the peace of Lancaster County. While living in Conestoga Manor, he became acquainted with a Peter Chartiere, a Shawanese half-breed, who was influential in getting Tobias Hendricks to live on the Indian lands. Even though the grounds were ideal for hunting and planting, by the time Cumberland County was formed, all of the Indians, including Chartiere, had wandered off to the Ohio. By this action, the Indians forfeited all claim to the Manor of Lowther, and it reverted to the proprietaries.

In 1765, a John Armstrong surveyed the area and divided it up into twenty-eight separate tracts, ranging from 150 to over 500 acres out of an aggregate of 7,551 total acreage.

In 1908, this section, the Manor of Lowther, was described this way:

Its uplands and slopes teem with rich harvests, thickly sprinkled with commodious farm buildings and comfortable beautiful modern homes, and the whole expanse is a delightful picture of industry, thrift, and plenty.

Map of Camp Hill development, 1891–1963. West Shore Country Club is situated at upper right in East Pennsboro Township.

THE WAR BETWEEN THE STATES AND THE STORY OF THE UNION DRUMMER BOY

During the last days of June 1863, one-third of General Robert E. Lee's Confederate Army was in Cumberland County preparing to lay siege to the Pennsylvania Capital City. Already having occupied Chambersburg, Carlisle, and Mechanicsburg, Lee's forces began to probe the Union Army defenses of Harrisburg. Confederate artillery set up on the high point of the Peace Church on Trindle Spring Road and shelled the area of the Oyster Point Tavern, where the Trindle Spring Road met the Carlisle-Harrisburg Pike at what is now Twenty-eighth and Market streets in Camp Hill.

Under the command of Confederate Cavalry General Albert Gallatin Jenkins, the "Johnny Rebs" had crossed the fields of the Samuel Bowman farm (now the West Shore Country Club) and captured a Union soldier as he rested on the porch of the farmhouse of his brother-in-law, George Oyster (on what is now Country Club Road). Earlier, a Union Army soldier had attempted to "liberate" a horse from the Bowman farm (later to become the first clubhouse of the West Shore Country Club). The West Shore area was the Confederate Army's furthest penetration of northern territory during the Civil War.

Samuel Bowman Farmhouse, around 1900

On the afternoon of June 29, 1863, General Robert E. Lee—headquartered in Chambersburg—sent orders to General Jenkins and his troops to abandon the planned capture of the lightly defended northern transportation and communications center of Harrisburg and head to a small town to the south and east. Lee had received word that the tens of thousands of troops of the Union Army—now under the command of General George Gordon Meade—were marching north out of Maryland into the farmlands of Pennsylvania. On June 30, 1863, Union Army troops, following

Bowman Family Geneology, 1733–1950s

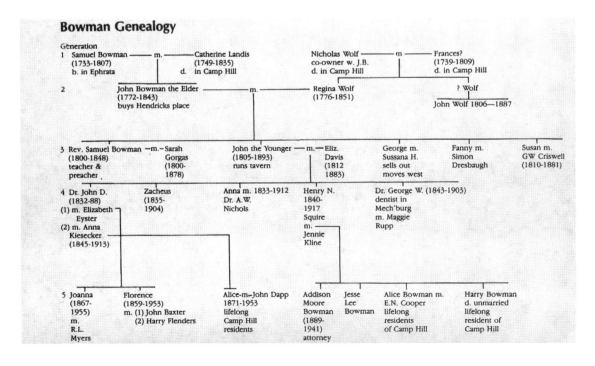

the Confederates down the Carlisle-Harrisburg Pike, encountered a force of rebels holed up in a stone barn. The resulting "Skirmish at Sporting Hill" left at least sixteen Confederates dead. The last Union Army soldier wounded in the military encounters on the west shore of Harrisburg was Morris Gerrits, a drummer boy with the New York State National Guard, 22nd Infantry Regiment. The great drama of Gettysburg began the next day.

There have been two distinctive graphics that have identified the West Shore Country Club. The West Shore Crest was suggested by a local advertising executive, Ed Michener, a Club president during the 1960s. He suggested that a crest be developed that should depict elements of the area's history.

When Michener began to research the property on which the Club is located, he found that the parcels were part of the original deeded land from William Penn. Subsequently, the West Shore Crest he created included a crown and the Penn family's coat of arms.

THE WSCC CREST AND LOGO

Bill Greenlee, Club president in 2006, had learned through research that a New York drummer boy in the Union Army became the Civil War's most northern casualty during the "Skirmish at Sporting Hill" near the Club. This occurred the day before the Battle of Gettysburg. The Confederacy's most northern excursion in 1863 was on the west shore of Harrisburg.

Thus, the Union Drummer Boy logo adorns Club gear and other materials.

—— 2 ——

A CLUB IS FORMED

Any organization that has succeeded over eighty years usually owes its beginnings to a person or small group of individuals who first established a foundation for building and expansion. That certainly was the case when a transplanted Brit was assigned to Central Pennsylvania to manage the Harrisburg agency of Aetna Casualty Insurance Company.

When Englishman Franklin Davies moved into a house at Twenty-fourth Street and the bypass in Camp Hill, the bachelor brought his furniture, clothing, and a cherished set of golf clubs—all with hickory shafts. He also brought with him a love for, if not an addiction to, golf, and began considering the options available for filling his spare hours with the game he loved. Now, 1928 was a heady time with the stock market spiraling upward and the paper rewards of investment being rapidly compounded. Davies found a small group of men who shared his interest in golf and they began meeting, first in homes and finally in the Camp Hill Fire House in March, to incorporate and draw up the by-laws for what we now know as the West Shore Country Club. The original incorporators—Edward H. Bower, Herman F. Keihl, John E. Myers, Carl K. Deen, and G. W. Ensign—traveled to Carlisle on March 28, 1928, to have a Cumberland County judge approve the by-laws and documents required to incorporate the West Shore Country Club.

Now, they had to find a suitable tract of land on which to build a nine-hole course. Two developers were commissioned to conduct the search until they secured an option on the

Franklin Davies

Aerial photograph of West Shore Country Club in 1939. Club property is at left. In the foreground is the strip known at the time as "the dirt road," now Route 11-15. At right is Christian L. Seibert Memorial Park.

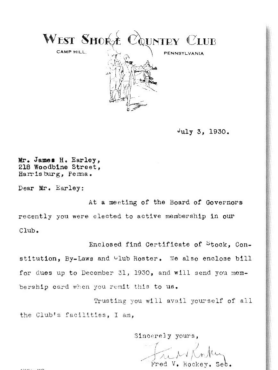

West Shore Country Club
CAMP HILL.   PENNSYLVANIA

July 3, 1930.

Mr. James H. Earley,
218 Woodbine Street,
Harrisburg, Penna.

Dear Mr. Earley:

At a meeting of the Board of Governors
recently you were elected to active membership in our
Club.

Enclosed find Certificate of Stock, Con-
stitution, By-Laws and Club Roster. We also enclose bill
for dues up to December 31, 1930, and will send you membership card when you remit this to us.

Trusting you will avail yourself of all
the Club's facilities, I am,

Sincerely yours,

Fred V. Rockey. Sec.

PVR:MS.

Left: *In April 1928, the newly formed West Shore Country Club published its governing documents.*

Right: *Mr. James Early received this letter from Club Secretary Fred Rockey welcoming his new membership.*

sixty-nine-acre Samuel Bowman farm, then in possession of the Hoopy family. The land was contoured perfectly for a golf course. A price of $14,700 was negotiated and the new by-laws stipulated that the Club membership would be limited to 225 persons; each member accepted would purchase one share of stock for one hundred dollars, and dues would be thirty-five dollars a year, with a twenty-five-dollar charge for females. The Carlisle Trust Company provided a $10,000 mortgage on the property, which included livestock. One of the first orders of business was to sell the horses and the wheat to buy a tractor. The second order of business was to pass a rule banning alcoholic beverages of any kind on Club property, in compliance with federal law. Members honored the rule by ignoring it.

The farmhouse—which was the birthplace of George Hoopy, the energetic Lemoyne insurance agent who eventually became one of the West Shore Country Club's oldest and most beloved members—soon became the clubhouse. After clearing the barn of hay, wheat, and some animals, the first meeting of the Board of Governors was held there in July; the founders and the original board members had been meeting weekly since incorporation and did so until November of that same year. George Morris—a descendent of Scotland's "Old Tom" Morris—was paid $125 to help design the first nine holes of the new golf course. At the time, Morris was the golf professional at the Colonial Country Club on ground that is now a shopping center. It would be 1929 before a work-in-progress nine holes were ready to play, while the tennis courts had been open since July 1928. The Club had served as a social gathering place while members waited for a golf course. In the fall of 1928, the Club purchased a Victrola music box for dances, but returned it when the treasury needed the money to heat the clubhouse over the winter.

Among the thirty-five women golfers of the West Shore Country Club who met at the clubhouse to outline the season's plans were, left to right, Mrs. John B. Lee, Mrs. Horace Selig, Mrs. William R. Hapgood, and Mrs. Charles Bushong.

Many renovations were to be completed in the farmhouse, including plumbing and decorating. It was fortuitous that all of this happened in 1928, because 1929 brought the stock market crash that plunged the country into a deep depression. Even though loans were difficult to come by, the reputations of those leading the West Shore Country Club were enough to secure loans to improve the clubhouse and barn. The Club ended its first year with 160 members and a modest bank account. However,

At the Family Picnic Day at the West Shore Country Club. Around the table are: Mrs. H. J. Selig, Mrs. Roy Keffer, Mrs. John Lee, William Wooters, Horace Selig, and George Wade, president of the Club.

A group of women members of the West Shore Country Club enjoying the beauty of their surroundings at the spring opening on a Saturday. From left to right are: Mrs. Don McGrew, Mrs. George N. Wade, Mrs. Lorin High, Mrs. John B. Lee, and Miss Lillian Wolfe.

as the economy faltered, the rate of delinquent dues payments accelerated. Early in 1930, with the Club's business feeling the impact of the economic slowdown, the Board voted to borrow $4,000 from a Camp Hill bank to remodel the clubhouse and rehabilitate the barn. The bank agreed to the loan, stipulating that every member of the Board co-sign the loan document. That ended that idea. Nevertheless, the Club entered 1931 with a cash balance of $637.07. It spent that and more on the delayed clubhouse remodeling and even entertained the purchase of ninety-five additional adjacent acres to the north for $13,500. The idea was vetoed, but a dues increase of ten dollars a year was passed.

Scotsman Jack Norrie was hired as the first golf professional for $125 a month for seven months. He stayed for five years. When the Prohibition ended in 1933, the Club secured a liquor license, allowing it to do what it had been doing all along, and the Club bade farewell to its founder, Franklin Davies, who had been transferred out of the area.

On March 31, 1906, Emanuel Hoopy, father of Harry Hoopy, purchased 101 acres of land and buildings from Theodore Eslinger for $11,500. The large stone farmhouse built in 1821 became the home of Harry Hoopy, a former teacher at the Lantz and West Fairview schools, and his wife, Martha Bretz, from the Enola area. On June 25, 1906, George Clayton Hoopy was born on this farm that in 1928 became the West Shore Country Club. He was named after a great uncle, George Hoopy, who fought in the Civil War from 1861 to 1864; during this time, he was captured by the Confederates and died in an Andersonville, Georgia prison in October 1864. George attended the former one-room Oyster School

GEORGE C. HOOPY

in East Pennsboro Township with all eight grades together. George would arise early to complete farm chores, then drive a horse, wagon, and his two sisters to that school. His job on the farm was to watch the cows for twenty-five cents a week. After his father passed away, his mother sold the farm for $20,250 to Theodore Eslinger and moved to Lemoyne, where George graduated from Lemoyne High School in 1924. After a few years working at Manbeck's Bakery and attending the Harrisburg Academy, he departed by train to attend a school of osteopathy in Philadelphia, but decided en route to continue to North Carolina, where he became a freshman at Duke University. In 1927, the total yearly tuition, including room and board, books, and fees, was about $300. While on campus, George served as president of the Phi Delta Theta fraternity, manager of the varsity tennis team, and vice-president of the Men's Association and Student Government. He was a member of the ODK National Honorary Leadership Fraternity. When he graduated from Duke in 1931, the yearbook carried this comment: "And even his failings leaned to virtue's side."

George Hoopy's first employment was with the Pennsylvania Department of Revenue as an inheritance tax inspector, and then to the Public Utilities Commission as supervisor of Common Carriers. In 1935, he started the Hoopy Insurance Agency in Lemoyne and retired in 1977. Interested in community betterment, George was one of the founders of the West Shore Businessmen's Association and then later served as president after it became the West Shore Chamber of Commerce. George became a member of the West Shore Country Club in 1949 and was Golf Committee chairman of the Board of Governors in the 1950s. He served as chairman of

the Cumberland County Housing Authority, vice president of the Redevelopment Authority, board member of Dauphin Deposit Trust Company, board member of the Navy League, served on the Board of Associates of Messiah College, was a member of the National Rifle Association, and was master of the West Shore Masonic Lodge No. 681. He served in the 104th Cavalry of the Pennsylvania National Guard and in the United States Air Force during World War II.

George was almost universally well liked. He played golf until he was one hundred years old and garnered a hole-in-one at the West Shore Country Club. He passed away on July 12, 2007, eight years after the death of his wife, Patricia. George Hoopy's legacy will be long remembered at the West Shore Country Club. A substantial sum of money was designated to the Club in his will, and a number of worthy projects were accomplished as a memorial to this gentleman, friend, philanthropist, golfer, humanitarian, and community-minded individual.

3

THROUGH THE YEARS

Since its beginning as a nine-hole course in 1928 and through the fifty years of its growth, the West Shore Country Club golf course has proven to be a true test of golf to many of the finest players in Central Pennsylvania and, on numerous occasions, the world's finest. It is a tribute to the foresight and energy of those early members of this Club that such is the case. Working with limited budgets and developing the Club through the lean years of the Depression, it is a wonder that they survived at all.

By 1936, thoughts of expanding the barn gave way to a zeal for clubhouse expansion and, finally, in 1938, with European storm clouds gathering, the Board began serious planning to add a ball-room, kitchen, and locker room at a cost not to exceed $10,000. The plans faltered because it was impossible to get the necessary financing. Then, in 1940, the Central Bank and Trust Company offered a loan of $30,000 at 5 percent interest, which enabled the Club to go forward with improvements and retire a $20,000 Carlisle Trust loan. The $10,000 grew to $15,000, but the improvements included a fireplace in the ballroom and showers in the basement. There was a gala dedication party in October. Franklin Davies returned for the event; the Board authorized an expenditure of two dollars for his overnight stay at the Penn Harris Hotel.

Four years after the land expansion idea had been rejected, it was revisited at the request of President Leon Metzger. With the ninety-five acres now offered at $10,000, the Board voted to expand the golf course to its current eighteen holes and closed the deal in October 1935. In later years, the Club chose not to acquire another large parcel of additional adjacent land that is now a residential development.

It is unclear when illegal slot machines made their first appearance at the Club, but they remained a not-to-be-talked-about basement feature of what came to be known as the "Black Hole of Calcutta" where cards were shuffled, drinks were on hand, and the

Children's party in the playground in front of the clubhouse, circa 1930

Left: *While men of the West Shore Country Club appropriated the golf course for opening day events, the women held a bridge tea at the clubhouse, with Mrs. Leon Metzger as chair. Engrossed in a hand above are, left to right, Miss Betsy Shank, Miss Alma Hull, Mrs. John B. Lee, and Mrs. Ralph Eppley.*

Right: *One table of bridge players caught by the camera as they chat after a rubber of bridge at a party at the West Shore Country Club. Left to right around the table are Mrs. Thomas L. Goss, Mrs. E. R. Hapgood, Mrs. Franklin Musser, and Mrs. John Lee.*

one-armed bandits contributed to the Club's income. The machines, scattered throughout Pennsylvania, were against an un-enforced state law that eventually brought a 1950s state police crackdown.

Despite the dragging economy, the Club determined to build the new nine holes at a three-hole-a-year pace, to be completed in 1938. Before the project was completed, the Borough of Camp Hill suggested that the Club—which sat in East Pennsboro Township—agree to be annexed. In one of its more astute decisions, the Board rejected the opportunity to give up its liquor license and become part of alcohol-free Camp Hill.

Into this party atmosphere, the blast from Pearl Harbor reverberated throughout the nation and into the West Shore Country Club. In early 1942, at the first meeting of the Board of Directors after the bombing, the Board members decided that all future meetings throughout the war would include the singing of the National Anthem. They also authorized the use of the clubhouse as a casualty station if necessary. Greens fees were decreased for military personnel, down to $1.50 for officers for weekends and holidays; enlisted men were invited to play golf for one dollar at any time. Three golf tournaments were held in 1942 to benefit the Red Cross. When Dr. Eufryn Jones resigned his Club membership to enter the army, his wife was granted social privileges during the duration of his enlistment. By 1943, out of 239 members, twenty had entered military service. The Board extended complimentary memberships to those enlisted men so that they had full access to the facilities while on leave. Of four brothers who caddied at the Club who all joined the military, one became a Japanese prisoner.

Rationing affected many areas of country club life. Bridge luncheons, once a frequent social occurrence at the Club, were scheduled for only once a month. Golf balls were in scarce

supply; only after turning in an old ball as partial payment, would it be replaced with a reprocessed one. Because of the gasoline shortage, a hay wagon was hired to provide those attending Saturday night parties with transportation; the cost for the evening was $1.65 per couple, including food. Even mowing and maintenance were strictly scheduled, due to rationing of resources. By 1947, Club membership was reinstated to those military members who had served and returned home. In 1949, the golf champion, John Weaver, Jr., who had returned from naval service with a serious leg injury, and had been outfitted with a metal brace, walked during his match. It was his fifth championship.

It was in 1943, during an October Board meeting, when Ed Tabor was hired as the pro and greenskeeper at a salary of $2,250, plus income from Club racks. At the time, he was also authorized to get a defense plant job as long as it did not interfere with his Club duties. His many years of service and dedication to the Club had far-reaching effects, unforeseen at the time.

Left: At the West Shore County Club, left to right are, Mrs. John B. Lee, Mrs. Thomas Goss, and Mrs. William R. Hapgood. Mrs. Hapgood is holding the flowers which she received in the bridge games after the golf and luncheon.

Right: Ripley's Believe It or Not featuring WSCC's Ollie Bunce, 1948

Members of the West Shore Country Club were hosts at a stag party in honor of all former servicemen of the Club. Included among the honored guests and officials in charge of the party were, seated, from left: Richard Tyner, W. Dixon Morrow, Robertson C. Cameron, J. Earl Bowman, Robert Shaw, Jr., W. L. Lampe, and J. B. Gillars. Standing, from left: Club Manager Donald McDonald, Edward Hill, William Wood, Jr., Hubert Manning, Fred McDonnell, Roland Knox, H. E. Pease, and Club President Harold B. Miller. Following the reception, a buffet supper was served and motion pictures were shown. The party was the first get-together for all former servicemen of the Club.

When the Club's liquor license was granted in 1946, it was decided that professional club management was needed. Mr. and Mrs. Donald McDonald were hired, having been recommended as highly experienced club managers. That move started the Club on the way toward profitability.

When, in 1948, the Club received a $100,000 mortgage to build a new clubhouse, it was decided that the McDonalds were not up to handling an expanded staff and broadened management responsibilities. The Board began to search for a new professional steward.

CHARLIE KNISLEY, CLUB MANAGER

Among the applicants interviewed were Charles Knisley, a native of Mifflintown who gained his club management experience as a manager of an officer's club in Miami, Florida. The Board offered Knisley a management contract that included family living quarters on the second floor of the clubhouse. Mr. and Mrs. McDonald graciously resigned upon Knisley's appointment.

Knisley's value to the Club became apparent in his first year. He acted as an advisor on the remodeling work on the clubhouse, particularly in the kitchen. He tightened controls over pilfering and waste. As a result of Knisley's efforts, the Club showed a profit of $8,000 in Knisley's first year as steward.

Charlie Knisley's astute management for over thirty years was largely responsible for the widespread community acceptance and success of the West Shore Country Club. Knisley did it all, sometimes doubling his duties as chef after an abrupt personnel change. He drove to Baltimore on a weekly basis to procure the finest and freshest seafood. West Shore Country Club's Crab Cake was known far and wide as the best in the area.

Knisley organized many social events. Most popular, in the 1960s and 1970s, were the trips he put together to Penn State football games. Forty or fifty Club members would gather in the morning and return for a celebratory dinner at the Club following the game.

In 1976, West Shore's clubhouse was set for another remodeling. Charlie Knisley took the lead. Near completion of the renovations, a contest was held with members to name various rooms. To honor the Club manager, the remodeled ballroom was named the Knisley Ballroom.

Charles M. Knisley, CCM, whose astute management for more than thirty years was largely responsible for the widespread community acceptance and success of the West Shore Country Club in its early years.

An early picture of the Knisley family, taken not long after Charlie assumed the role of Club manager. The family actually lived on Club property for several years.

Dedication of the new facilities took place on March 25, 1977, with an event attended by more than 400 members and called Knisley Night in honor of Mr. Knisley and his wife Marge. The couple was presented with a trip to Europe as a token of appreciation for his skill and dedication in helping make the Club such an outstanding success over so many years.

By 1950, what was to become a time of growth for the West Shore Country Club and a tumultuous decade for our country was ushered in with a gala black-tie party in the ballroom. The cost was fifteen dollars a couple and included dinner, a floor show, and breakfast. Our nation was once again involved in conflict, this time in Korea, a place unknown to so many of those conscripted for duty. President Harry S. Truman called it a police action, but in reality, it was a war orchestrated by China encouraging North Korea to invade its sister country to the south with the promise that if the going got tough, the Chinese would cross the Yalu River and engage any who fought for South Korea. In 1952, General Dwight D. Eisenhower ran on a campaign pledge that, if elected, he would go to Korea and find a way to end the war. Indeed, that is what happened, and the country and our Club embarked on a period of growth, development, and prosperity.

Lee Stouffer remembers that after World War II, when the Shore Room was built, the Club came alive with members "living" there each day until early the next morning. The proceeds from the slot machines helped pay for the new facility. Many came to watch their favorite television programs; televised pro football was rare, but brought in the people on Sunday. A glass of beer was ten cents for a ten-ounce glass, the lunch special was eighty-five cents, and the Five O'Clock Club was popular to watch with Larry Yost and that gang. Many events were hosted: pig roasts, crab feasts, and such. Women also enjoyed a few beers in the Shore Room after a round of golf. Lee remembers Lib Latham, his mother Lucky Stouffer, Isabel Town, and Berth Straights. Says Lee, "One time I overheard a conversation that went like this:

'Don't you think we should go home and fix dinner for the men?'

'To hell with the men,' was the reply."

Top: *25th Anniversary Dinner-Dance held January 14, 1955*

After that, they named themselves the West Shore Home Wreckers Club.

In 1950, the Board authorized the purchase of a two-ton air conditioning system and what a relief it was on those humid summer days. The cost was $810. Another critical decision was made in July, when at a special meeting, a Mr. Saul offered property he owned—8.7 acres along the No. 12 fairway—to the Club for $25,000. A member of the Board appraised the land to be worth $16,800, and the offer was rejected. The land was subsequently subdivided, and the lots were sold individually to become a housing development.

Clubhouse photo from 1950. Taken from where the current pool is located.

Entrance fees were one hundred dollars for active membership in 1951, and a "stag and doe" was held one Saturday evening. Meanwhile, U.S. Senator Joseph R. McCarthy held the nation spellbound with his assertions that there were Communist agents throughout all of government, but, in the end, the senator was unable to produce enough legal evidence to support a single charge. In 1952, serious planning began for what was to become a great asset for the Club—a swimming pool. Initial cost estimates were $70,000, financed by a twenty-five-dollar dues increase, but the 1953 annual meeting rejected the proposal. Flytraps for the clubhouse were approved at that meeting, along with a tree-planting program to encompass the next five years, and hopefully yield 10,000 trees.

Perhaps the best news of 1953 was the acceptance of Dr. Alex McKechnie as an active member, and in 1954, active dues

The old pool in 1955

increased from forty dollars a year to $140. Family memberships in the planned pool could be purchased by buying a one-hundred-dollar non-interest bond and agreeing to an annual fee of fifty dollars in addition to regular dues. The pool was to be dedicated in July of 1955, but was postponed for a year.

The Club received a gracious letter from President Eisenhower in appreciation for his honorary membership. He subsequently teed it up and enjoyed his round on our friendly but challenging course. It was said that a distinguishing characteristic of the West Shore Country Club is that the average golfer is capable of shoot-

ing par on any hole, but there are no "gimmees."

Golf Chairman George Hoopy decided in 1956 to increase the fee for playing in weekend tournaments to ten dollars from seven dollars and fifty cents. A committee was appointed to look into a possible new site for the clubhouse. The putting green was installed in 1957 and the Russians launched *Sputnik*—again placing a huge challenge in front of our country's leaders.

The USGA gave the course a rating of seventy in 1958, and on July 25, 1959, there was a memorable golf exhibition by Arnold Palmer, Governor Dick Schleichter, Art Wall, and our venerable pro, Ed Tabor. The charge was one dollar and profits after expenses went to the Ladies Auxiliary of Harrisburg Osteopathic Hospital.

Meanwhile, Marilyn Monroe became the nation's number one sex symbol, teenagers were captivated by the afternoon show *American Bandstand,* and Disneyland was flourishing, a result of the "imagineering" instituted by its founder who brought us such things as Tomorrowland, Fantasyland, and Frontierland, to name a few. But for West Shore Country Club members, the Club was a special place indeed to spend one's leisure hours for dining or recreational pleasures.

Alex J. McKechnie, DDS and his family moved to Camp Hill in 1953, where he opened a general practice of dentistry.

Within a few months, he submitted his application for membership into the West Shore Country Club, at which time the entrance fee was $300. Alex has always been interested in helping to further the growth and betterment of the Club. He was elected to the Board of Governors in 1960, and was then elected to the position of secretary in 1964 and served in that position for thirty-six years.

ALEX McKECHNIE

Because Alex served as unofficial photographer and producer of the Club's publication, *Par*, for many years, we have hundreds of old photos and memories from which to draw.

Alex's kind demeanor and jovial attitude soon won many friends. Alex was a good friend to many, but with none better than George Hoopy. In fact, Hoopy sought Alex's counsel when deciding to bequeath some of his estate to the Club.

Alex was named secretary emeritus when he retired from that office and was honored by his peers with honorary membership and a lifelong position on the Executive Committee and the Board of Governors, where his institutional memory has proven invaluable.

He was further honored by having his name added to the name of an annual West Shore members' tournament that is now called the Alex J. McKechnie Member-Member Golf Tournament, played annually at West Shore Country Club. Because Alex was an avid golfer and is still a student of the game, it is most appropriate that this event bears his name. The Alex J. McKechnie Member-Member Golf Tournament is one of the truly fun events at the Club that he and good friend Foster Hopkins won in 1993. Competition in the two-day event is keen. However, the tournament features the "Great West Shore Shoot-Out," offering lots of laughs, and it is a wonderful time for couples to visit and enjoy each other's company; and that's what West Shore and Alex McKechnie are all about.

Coincidentally, in 1939, when Dr. Alex graduated from Bloomsburg State Teachers College, West Shore Country Club past president Nelson Swarts was born in Bloomsburg Hospital, just across the street from the graduation ceremonies.

"Dr. Alex," as he is known, receives recognition from 2008 West Shore president Henry Line.

1960s – DECADE OF CHANGE

During the 1960s, the West Shore Country Club was in a period of continued prosperity as it began its transition into one of the finest members' country clubs in the Commonwealth. Life was fairly routine on the west shore, even while the tumultu-

Getting ready to tee off in 1964

ous newspaper headlines announced turmoil: the national mourning for Martin Luther King, Jr., John F. Kennedy, and Robert Kennedy, who all fell to assassins' bullets; the Russians building the Berlin Wall and their invasion of Czechoslovakia; and the escalation of the conflict in Vietnam. On a brighter, yet still chaotic, side, The Beatles toured the U.S., while on our west coast, the music of the Beach Boys delighted our sense of sound. The West Shore Country Club opened the decade of the sixties with 462 active members: twenty-seven Female, eighty-two Social, twelve Junior, and three Retired.

The philosophy of the West Shore Country Club was articu-lated by the Green Committee in 1963: "A really good golf course should challenge the skill of the exceptional golfer, but not penalize the average golfer, and provide maximum enjoyment for all." And so began an improvement project—often thwarted

Summer "Jockey" Party, 1960

by the forces of nature and the forces of personality—to implement this maxim. First up was a tree-planting program, which provided 140 evergreens to be dispersed about the course, and an additional half-dozen hardwoods. A few of these trees yet remain—those that weren't later sacrificed for further, different, improvements, or lost to drought. At No. 9, a new pond was dug, graded, and filled with water, and named "Bowman's Lake," which the resident muskrat population celebrated by building an intricate web of underground tunnels.

By 1964, the fairways had become dry and hard, with vast sections of reddish brown knotweed and brown areas where poa annua died. The golfers were unhappy, venting their displeasure to the Golf Committee during the extremely hot summer drought. There was no grass to cut for weeks and the grounds crew spent their time working on the new maintenance shed. By the following year, the installation of a new watering system became a priority, which included dredging the lake to increase the Club's water storage capacity and installing a sprinkler system—at a cost of $50,400. Robert Trace provided needed assistance and intervention with the Water Power and Resources Board with the location and use of a pumping station. The excavation was through twenty-two feet of solid rock. As a result of this new watering and fertilization program, the fairways were mowed ninety-eight times, twice as often as in 1964. The next year, the lake was excavated five feet deeper to increase water storage capacity and retard algae growth. Soon, the course was lush and green, with both pumps operating concurrently. This created a very high stand-by demand and an invoice of $1,724 from Pennsylvania Power & Light for one year of electric service. The Club had signed a five-year contract for a minimum of $568 per year. The Liaison Committee met with the electric company representatives, and managed to obtain a $554 rebate. Consequently, Riley Heckert was instructed to operate only one pump at a time to obtain a more favorable electric rate. Even with the new system in place, another severe winter and drought caused the course to suffer its poorest conditions in many years.

Even so, the course became host to many exhibitions and special matches over the course of the decade; some noteworthy, like the match that wasn't. In 1961, Arnold Palmer almost participated in an exhibition golf match with Gary Player on a bright, friendly Wednesday afternoon, but the cost was determined to be prohibitive, so much so that the idea was "knocked into a cocked hot" (according to the minutes), even after discussing several options: $7,500 to the Palmer-Players Enterprises to one-third of the revenues going to the Club and two-thirds to the participants. It didn't happen.

In 1962, Dick Jordan, who would later become president of the Club, aced No. 9; Jim Tabor, Ed Tabor's son and an accomplished amateur player, who later would win several men's golf championships, had the distinction of winning the Beaten 8s championship flight; and Dixon Earley, currently the secretary of the Club, and also a past president, won the fifth flight Beaten 8s—the humble beginnings of a lifetime of distinguished accomplishments on the golf course. In 1965, in the teen golf championship, the winner of the Beaten 8s was Kipp Stecher, later the CEO of the Americhoice Credit Union and the 1966 Junior Club champion, adding to the list of inauspicious starts. To further help along the distinguished golfers, in 1965, the "flag stick option" rule, whereby the flag stick could remain in the hole without penalty as long as the ball is at least the length of the flag stick away from the hole, was approved by the Board of Governors.

In January 1963, the Board voted unanimously to extend Club privileges to the governor of Pennsylvania, The Honorable William W. Scranton, and his immediate family, for the duration of his tenure as governor. In May, the same invitation was extended to Lieutenant Governor Raymond P. Shafer.

Staffing the West Shore Country Club was no small feat, requiring many delicate negotiations. In 1963, at a special three-hour meeting on October 8, the Board discussed the intended resignation of Manager Knisley, who, for personal and financial reasons, planned to terminate his employment on November 1 to accept the manager position at the York Country Club. Despite several recesses and a five-year counter offer, Mr. Knisley's resignation was accepted with regret and then-president Colestock appointed an applicant screening committee. A week later, at the regular October 15 meeting, the Board proposed a five-year contract for Mr. Knisley, a $12,500 salary, a Christmas bonus of $500, personal dry cleaning, and food from the Club for his wife and son (a $2,000 value). Although he had signed a contract with the York Country Club, Knisley stated that his personal problems were resolved and his financial difficulties not as great

as he first imagined; therefore, he accepted the new West Shore
Country Club offer. The motion carried with three dissenting
votes and the screening committee was dismissed.

When the houseman and his wife stated their intention to
leave, their annual salary of $6,300 was increased $100 per month,
at a time when new teachers in the local school district were earn-
ing $4,000 a year. In 1964, one chef suddenly left; the replacement
would not show up in "fit condition" to work for two weeks at a
time. Manager Knisley acted as chef for a two-month period until
December, when a new chef was hired. In the meantime, he taught
the dishwashers how to cook. By 1969, advertisements for employment at the West Shore Country Club were cancelled due to the fact
that no one was applying. To retain help,
an across-the-board increase was granted
for the first time in the Club's history.

The freewheeling "let it all hang
out" mantra of the sixties meandered
through the nation, and made its way
onto the grounds of the West Shore
Country Club. In 1962, a Board
member inquired as to the proper
length of shorts on women. Another
governor wanted to examine the nature
of the complaint, whether this was a
"case of too-long shorts or too-short
shorts." In 1962, non-Club members
"crashed" teen-aged swimming parties.
Local police were employed to curb
their attendance. By 1964, trespassing
by children and adults had become a
serious and growing problem. A fence

*Aerial photo in the 1970s showing
considerable development since the
1930s. The old pool is still in the
photo at left and "new" tennis courts
are in place.*

was considered. The fourth green was seriously damaged by
vandals with sand rakes. Complaints of profanity by individuals in
the Shore Room brought warnings from the House Committee
and the manager. In 1966, the Club itself hosted a mini-rebellion of
its own. The USGA disapproved of the Calcutta stag, but the Board
approved it on July 15. Meanwhile, the Vietnam War hung like
a gloomy cloud. In 1962, Lieutenant Jay Cleveland, at that time
a Junior Member, was placed on a leave of absence for 1963 for
military service. Later, the entrance fee was waived for vets.

This was also a time of big-name entertainment at the club-house. In 1963, one of the first color televisions in the area was purchased for the Shore Room. Members came to watch television in the evenings, forming a group of regulars who came to watch their favorite shows. In 1967, an eggnog party drew 1,000 guests. In 1968, the Tommy Dorsey supper-dance had excellent reviews, but the Club did not make any money. As a result, the Count Basie party was cancelled. The following year, the band was invited back for a dinner-dance; this was the first time the Club made money with a "big name" band. To prepare for the event, the dining room was closed at 3 p.m. so that the kitchen could concentrate on preparing for the dinner-dance that evening. Later that year, the Glen Miller Orchestra had a moderate attendance and was a "break even" financial event.

Tensions often flourished among the state and its road-building projects, the Club members who desired exclusiveness, and the Club members who desired expansion of the facilities. In 1962, golf outings by outside groups were restricted to Tuesdays and Fridays. By 1969, the Board voted to eliminate all "outside" golfing parties between May 1 and October 1 of each year. All golf parties sponsored by a member were limited to four foursomes and play was restricted to Tuesdays and Fridays. Over the course of the next few decades, they were further restricted to only a couple a year, and these were to benefit Hospice of Central PA.

In 1966, a Planning Committee was proposed by the president and approved by the Board to be composed of past presidents, an architect, a builder, engineers, an attorney, and the treasurer. They were charged with creating a five- to ten-year overall plan for the Club. Later that year, the architects' fee of 7.5 percent was accepted. It included preliminary plans, working drawings, and project supervision. The total cost of the interior work was expected to be $300,000 (later increased to $380,222) but was reduced to $225,000 when the kitchen improvements were "ruled out for now." The major remodeling of the clubhouse included an enlarged men's locker room, new shower room, sauna bath, men's bar, new frozen food lockers, enlarged ballroom, new enlarged kitchen quarters, main

Tommy "The Bartender" Hoffman's genial personality and stories about his beloved Yankees kept members entertained throughout the sixties and seventies. Tommy would not serve young boys "Shirley Temples"; he gave them "Mickey Mantles"!

entrance portico, new quarters for the building superintendent, additional office spaces, and new restrooms. The work was contracted in 1967 and completed in 1968. During the completion of the building program, a temporary kitchen was set up by Manager Knisley for two months: May and June. In July, the kitchen was moved "downstairs." The new kitchen opened on September 1.

They're Going to Build it Where?

In 1967, through the efforts of Dick Jordan and John Dietz (Club president in 1971), the No. 1 green was not included in the state's plans for the new road from the bypass to Brentwater Road. The Department of Highways's (now PennDOT) original plan would have devoured the No. 1 green, No. 2 tee, a large portion of the No. 1 fairway, and the entire practice fairway. The secretary of highways at the time, who would later become a Club member, was, perhaps not insignificantly, a tennis player, not a golfer. After considerable discussion with the agency, the current intersection of routes 11 and 15 and Brentwater Road was constructed with a turning lane starting at Country Club Road.

In 1968, the Board was offered the opportunity to purchase one hundred acres of ground across the Conodoquinet Creek off the No. 15 tee at $5,000 an acre with an option of $500 for one year. The motion to accept the offer was defeated with arguments that "we should forget expansion" and "reduce the membership." That same year, the Planning Committee projected plans for a "new clubhouse further out in the country." A 427-acre parcel under review was for immediate option at $800 per acre with a ten-year buy-out plan. By 1968, the total value of the West Shore Country Club property was determined to be $1,050,000.

THE 1970s – MAY YOU LIVE IN INTERESTING TIMES

At the West Shore Country Club, the decade of the seventies is remembered as a time of a changing environment. The decade heralded in the era of tennis at the Club. Improvements were made to the golf course as well. Also during the 1970s, West Shore Country Club leadership started to look toward the future in many aspects of the Club.

The decade began with the annual meeting on January 26, 1970; 125 active members were in attendance. The following were elected: James K. Thomas, president; John R. Dietz, vice

Top: *WSCC Swim Team, 1969*

Bottom: *WSCC Swim Team, 1972*

president; Richard T. Tyner, treasurer; and Dr. Alex J. McKechnie, secretary. The Board of Governors (three-year terms) included: John E. Farnham, Carlton E. Hughes, Jr., and Ed K. Smith.

At the annual meeting, the main topics of discussion by those in attendance were the need for tennis courts (holes No. 9, No. 14, and No. 18 were considered as locations) and problems with snowmobiling and tobogganing on the golf course. A dues increase of about 12 percent passed with very little dissension or opposition. Areas under consideration for some new tennis courts included the No. 18 fairway, the old equipment shed concrete pad, and the area in the vicinity of the practice green.

The tennis era began when a motion was approved in July 1972 to construct two tennis courts at an estimated cost of $24,000 in the area of the pitching green/fairways and a pitching green restructured between the No. 10, No. 8, and No. 1 fairways to be constructed for completion for the 1973 season. The construction of tennis courts had failed on several previous occasions. So, President Les Conner called for a special meeting of the membership to discuss the proposition. Since "only tennis players showed up for the meeting" (as it was recorded later), the

motion passed easily. So, in February 1973, the Board authorized the construction of two tennis "pods" at a cost not to exceed $50,000 on the site of the then current pitching green. Metered lights (twenty-five cents per hour) were to be installed. An electric power line was run from Country Club Road to serve the tennis courts. In June, Hempt Brothers was awarded a $47,000 contract to build four tennis courts. The final bill was $45,000. In 1974, Chuck Fromer was the first Tennis Club champion in the men's division and Carol Beatty was the first Tennis Club champion in the women's division. A new tennis pro shop was located in the old golf pro shop.

Dubious and Bizarre Events During the Seventies

The turbulence of the 1960s spilled over into the 1970s as far as the country club was concerned. Vandalism ran rampant during the decade. For instance, in 1970, some motorcycles used the No. 5 tee as a hill climb and a four-wheel-type vehicle caused damage to the No. 14 and No. 15 fairways. During the Christmas holidays, vandals with an automobile tore up the No. 2,

No. 4, No. 7, No. 8, and No. 1 fairways. In addition, the No. 3 and No. 11 greens were damaged. In February, someone stole one of the new chairs from the lobby. The tall pipe green marker behind the No. 10 green was snapped off and the No. 16 green was damaged. It took ten man-days to repair and clean up the rash of vandalism to the golf course and shelters the week of April 2. In 1973, vandalism included the restrooms and maintenance center. Gasoline was siphoned from vehicles and the gasoline pump. On a Saturday in January 1975, smoke bombs were hurled into the lobby and stairs of the Club, and vandals broke into the maintenance shed and damaged several mechanisms in an apparent search for gasoline. Finally, in 1975, vandals completely dismantled the side rails of the bridge at No. 13, wrecked the insides of the restrooms on the golf course, and damaged the No. 5 green and a number of fairways and traps. But even vandalism did not compare to the damage inflicted by Tropical Storm Agnes in 1972.

Collection Issues and Thefts

A Democratic Party account of $8,000 due in January 1, 1971, received a partial payment of $3,000 in December 1971 with the balance finally received in February 1972 after numerous prodding letters and communications by phone to the former governor leader and party officials.

A former chef illegally charged $1,000 to the Club for personal merchandise he purchased. The matter was turned over to the East Pennsboro Township police and court action. Horace A. Johnson later represented the Club in court.

One year, $2,144 was stolen from the night deposit. Required repairs to doors, locks, desks, and a new safe amounted to an insurance reimbursement of $2,481. After the robbery, a burglar alarm system costing $1,000 was installed at the Club. A sofa and two chairs were stolen from the clubhouse. The furniture was recovered from the apartment of a work-release inmate of the State Correctional Institute in Camp Hill. In 1973, shoes kept disappearing from the men's locker room, baffling waiter/shoe attendant/Shore Room "czar" Harold Speaks. Bob Latham recalls that Speaks used to refer to him as "Little Ugly" and his father as "Big Ugly." "Here comes Big Ug and Little Ug," he would say.

Oil Crisis Hits Home

The 1973 oil crisis began on October 17, 1973, when the members of the Organization of Arab Petroleum Exporting Countries (OAPEC, consisting of the Arab members of OPEC plus Egypt and Syria) announced, as a result of the ongoing Yom Kippur War, that they would no longer ship oil to nations that had supported Israel in its conflict with Syria, Egypt, and Iraq (the United States, its allies in Western Europe, and Japan). The oil crisis was further exacerbated by government price controls in the United States. This scarcity is remembered best by the rationing of gasoline at service stations, with motorists facing long lines at gas stations. At the Club, the gasoline shortage caused a longtime supplier to cancel the Club's contract, which meant that the Club had to scramble for fuel to run its equipment.

Continued Improvements to the Property

Wes Burns, a member of the Planning Committee, gave recommendations for tennis courts, shoring up the corner of the barn structure, and increasing the number of parking spaces by re-lining the lots. A five-year rotating system allocating up to $30,000 per year for regular maintenance and repairs for the Shore Room, cocktail lounge, men's bar room, and the Shore Room kitchen was scheduled to begin in 1972. During the year, improvements to the facility included forty new trees, which were placed at strategic spots on the golf course. The entrance area to the Shore Room was renovated. Jim Romano supervised

a project to stop a leak in the dam that had turned a portion of the No. 14 fairway into a bog.

A new footbridge was installed at No. 8. An alternate tee was constructed at No. 5. The No. 2 green was recontoured. The No. 9 tee was made three-tiered to permit placements from 150 to 190 yards to the hole. The No. 2 green was rebuilt. Over 1,100 feet of new cart paths were placed.

To eliminate the possibility of additional damages to the front portico, a seventeen-inch green scalloped drape was installed around the edge of the canopy with West Shore Country Club painted thereon at a cost of $225.

New furniture and a new Oriental-style carpet were purchased for the front entrance. Les Conner recalls asking a member's spouse what she thought of the new entrance.

"It looks like a French whorehouse," she opined.

"How do you expect me to know what one looks like?" Les retorted.

By 1974, the firm of Bogar and Bink began some feasibility studies of several major and minor construction problems the Club "must face in the not-too-distant future" including short- and long-range goals. Included were the Shore Room, card room, storage room, and the main lounge. On December 5, 1974, a contract was signed with Bogar and Bink to design, remodel, and renovate certain existing areas and construct various additions to the country club. Contracts were awarded to Miller and Norford, Inc., for the remodeling and construction.

In 1972, dues for the year were: Active $400; Social $275; Female $225; Junior $225; and Retired $5. Entry fees were: Active $600; Female $400; Social $450; and Junior $300.

Mr. Tabor's contract salary was $5,220 per year. He was to be "on duty" from March 15 to December 15. He received eighteen dollars per bag, plus three dollars per pull cart storage. He was authorized to charge four dollars per half an hour for lessons. Retirement was to be mandatory at age sixty-five. He was to maintain a fleet of twenty-six carts with one dollar and fifty cents per round given to the Club.

Starting time "slips" replaced the old Wednesday phone call system. Times could be requested a week in advance. The rise of the computer age allowed handicaps to become computerized free of charge by Mr. Greg Sutliff's company, eliminating the old individual calculations by members of the committee.

The July 4th dinner-dance with the Covington Band cost twenty dollars per couple. The Club lost money "under the Club's bookkeeping system."

A proposal to install a TV set in the Shore Room was rejected by the Board.

Do you remember caddies at West Shore? Caddy fees were three dollars and fifty cents per bag for eighteen holes for Class A and three dollars per bag for eighteen holes for Class B. Class A caddies were generally the older kids who could carry two bags and keep up.

One year, five half-price nights brought out 534 people. The average liquor bill was eighty-one cents per person.

The waiting time from Social Transfer to Active was twenty-one months.

The cost per team for the member-guest tournament was ninety dollars.

Self-propelled carts (a.k.a. "Kangaroo Caddies"), except those owned by the Club, were banned from Club property. This policy stayed in place for thirty years until it was rescinded in 2005.

"Let's Dance!"

"Put on your red shoes and dance…" David Bowie made the song popular in the 1980s, but it applied to the 1970s as well. The Club held numerous dances, which were well attended. During the 1970s, due to its popularity, the Christmas formal dinner-dance was closed to Club members and their guests only—a tradition that lives on today. The president (by tradition) was the chairman of the Christmas dance and the vice president was in charge of the Thanksgiving dance. A dance was scheduled each month of the year. The Opening Day dinner-dance was the hosting responsibility of the Board of Governors. One hundred and seventy persons attended the 1973 Opening Day dinner-dance at the bargain price of seven dollars and fifty cents per person. The band cost $650 and cocktails were half-price. The Memorial Day dinner-dance cost fifteen dollars per couple with 250 in attendance. Toward the end of the decade, the Entertainment Committee recommended cutting the number of attendees and concentrating on a few. Still, that year, there were 140 persons at the Thanksgiving dinner-dance, 175 at the Oktoberfest, 250 at the Christmas formal, 100 celebrated New Year's at the Club, and 1,000 were at the annual Eggnog Party.

You Have to Get Me Into the Eggnog Party!

The Eggnog Party: everyone in Camp Hill and the surrounding areas knew that it meant the annual Christmas Eve gathering at the West Shore Country Club. While other parties drew 175 or 250, one year, the annual Eggnog Party saw 1,000 members and guests cram into the Club ballroom. It got so out-of-control that the Club issued a strict edict by 1978 that "no outside guests were permitted, members and visiting family only." This, of course, made it all the more desirable to get in for non-member friends of Club members—mainly those ages eighteen to twenty-two. Why? Because it became *the* place for returning college students, home for Christmas, to make contact with their high school buddies, share a drink and a laugh, and make plans for holiday break fun.

The festivities began at 4:30 p.m. and ended at 7 p.m.; or, rather, the bar closed at 7 p.m. Sparky, the portly African-American head waiter, dressed as Santa Claus, greeted the revelers at the entranceway with a thunderous, "Merry Christmas!" The entrance hall was jammed. Early arrivals got some of the mountain of shrimp. Eggnog (not virgin) was free; other drinks were not. Underage teens got older brothers to sneak them a rum and Coke. Everyone was in a festive mood. It was cocktail hour, the holiday chores and present buying were done, the kids and family were home and having fun with their friends, and everyone was relaxed. It was the gathering place before Christmas Eve church or dinner or both. It was the place to be on Christmas Eve.

A Heritage of Sound Financial Management

During the seventies, the fiscal year was changed to commence on October 1 and end on September 30. The Club went to an "all charge" system. A system of accrual accounting was instituted by the treasurer, John Plesic. Plesic also instituted funded depreciation to better portray the Club's net worth.

A Personnel Committee was established with George Patterson as appointed chairman. The EUR Datacenter implemented a system for processing payroll, accounts receivable, and general ledger accounting.

The Board established a "Capital Improvement Reserve Fund" with all assessments and initiation fees placed in that fund for the specific purpose of capital expenditures, replacements, improvements, and amortization of debts as a result of any capital expenditures.

Diving into the pool in the 1970s

A new special finance committee was appointed to review financial reports and offer suggestions on financial matters. It still operates today.

Changes and Renovations to the Golf Course

An enlarged No. 9 tee was brought to grade and sodded with Merion blue grass with the final touches to be made in the spring of 1973. Study was given to developing a new No. 14 hole, make the present No. 14 the No. 15 hole, and eventually release the No. 18 hole for other Club purposes. The No. 11 green was considered for renovation. A pitching green was proposed to be located between the No. 10 tee, No. 11 fairway, and the No. 8 fairway. It was never built; to this day, the Club lacks a sufficient short game practice area with the putting green and target greens sometimes doubling as chipping greens.

Mr. Derr Carpenter was requested to prepare and submit a proposal to rebuild the golf course with estimated associated costs. A 1964 recommendation from Dr. J. Harper from Penn State University (after the installation of a fairway watering system) advising that the lawn be converted to bent grass was concluded as not needed. As a result, by 1972 the fairways were predominantly poa annua ecology (98 percent). Then, in 1973, Penn State University agronomist and turf specialist Dr. J. Harper returned to outline various proposals for poa annua control programs on WSCC greens and fairways.

In July, a modified fairway rehabilitation program implemented by Mr. Liska brought grassless fairways; selective chemicals applications to kill the poa annua; carts restricted to the rough only (no crossing of fairways); balls moved to the rough from the fairways for play; the fairways were thatched, aerified, and dragged with chains; the No. 13 green received an accelerated poa annua eradication chemical program; and fairway No. 8 was so badly infested with crabgrass that chemicals were required to eradicate it.

Once the fairways were bare, bent, and blue, the perennial rye grass seed was heavily planted, accompanied by appropriate fertilizers. The seeding was done in three directions. The total cost of the program was estimated to be no more than $30,000.

A ranger was hired at two dollars per hour to patrol the golf course during the rehabilitation program to call attention to violations and report abuses. Only four members were issued warnings

Scott Stoner and Scott Christie prepare to compete in the 1976 Ed Tabor Invitational.

as the membership was most cooperative and understanding during this trying period. A "Sand-in-the-Traps" controversy ended when no new sand was purchased and the project was abandoned due to the prohibitive cost. As a compromise, the traps at No. 1 were reconstructed, drainage was placed, and the situation reevaluated during the spring of 1975.

The Ed Tabor Annual Invitational Tournament Established

In 1972, after many years of competition, the annual inter-club matches were cancelled due to the withdrawal of Colonial and Lebanon country clubs from the four-team format. The Carlisle and West Shore country clubs continued the tradition.

A proposal to schedule a Tabor District Tournament for 1975, to be sponsored by West Shore Country Club with the State Capital Savings and Loan Bank, failed on a vote of six to four. Then on Sunday, September 8, 1974, an Ed Tabor Day Tournament and Testimonial Dinner-Dance were scheduled with the participants limited to West Shore Country Club members. George Patterson chaired the event.

The first district Ed Tabor Better Ball Tournament was held August 21 through 24 and was co-chaired by Reg Seavey and George Patterson. It was an outstanding success. The State Capital Savings and Loan Association was a low-key financial supporter. Thirty-five years later, the Tabor Tournament is one of just a few invitational tournaments. It sells out weeks before the event.

Golf Notables

The East Pennsboro High School Golf Team was granted golfing privileges for nine practice dates and three matches.

In 1974, President Hank Johnson defeated Bob Wrightstone for his first Club championship at West Shore Country Club. These men frequently teamed together and won numerous district crowns. Hank Johnson was the only Club president to win the Club championship as president. Also that year, the District Junior Golf Tournament was won by Scott Christie. He also won the "Most Improved Golfer" award at West Shore Country Club. Christie went on to win fourteen Club championship titles and many district championships over a very successful amateur career.

In 1975, Ed Tabor was named Club Professional of the Year by the Philadelphia District PGA. In 1974 and 1975, Rusty

Miller was the Ladies Club champion. She would win nearly a dozen crowns throughout her career.

Yes, at West Shore Country Club, the seventies were a time of moving forward. Tennis began again at the Club. The seeds of renovation to the golf course and clubhouse, which would bloom in the future, were planted in the 1970s.

1980s—CONTINUED PROGRESS

The 1980s saw continuing improvements to the clubhouse, the golf course, the swimming pool, and the tennis courts. During the early part of the decade, numerous renovations and modifications improved the existing clubhouse to accommodate the increased use of the "old" clubhouse. In 1982, the House Committee noted that they were spending considerable time and monies on "numerous items of deterioration of this old clubhouse to keep it from falling down." In 1984, the Board hired the architectural firm of Bogar and Bink to provide a preliminary study of the future needs of the Club. In July, Bogar and Bink recommended the addition of significant additional storage areas, a pro shop,

Joe Gribb, Whitey Zerby, Johnny Johnson, and Walter Lutz in 1984

tennis shop, women's locker room, and new food management operations. Under consideration was either a new clubhouse, or a one-million-dollar expansion of the existing facility.

In 1985, the Planning Committee was presented with a plan for building a new main clubhouse on the site of the existing facility. The committee rejected the plan in favor of consideration of a new three-tiered office/pro shop/cart building on the "barn" site. The Board of Governors determined that the present structure be the "permanent" housing of the West Shore Country Club. At the annual meeting of the membership in 1986, the members approved a modified construction program, which was begun shortly thereafter. The "Great Remodeling and Reconstruction" project included enlargements to the Shore Room, Shore Room kitchen, ladies' lounge, men's lounge, locker rooms, pro shop, a storage area, and construction of a new tennis shop. In addition, a new stone entrance was constructed with new landscaping placed around it.

Improvements and upgrades to the golf course were issues of constant concern to the membership during the 1980s. Golf bunkers were added or expanded throughout, and many of the greens and tees were modified in an effort to make the course as challenging as possible. In 1989, a special Golf Course Improvement Committee created a ten-year plan with accompanying financial implications, which was adopted and implemented by the Board.

The 1980s saw many innovations and changes to the operation of the golf course. The Melex carts were replaced by the EZ-go units in 1981. Additionally, the stimpmeter (an instrument used to measure the "speed" of the greens) was introduced. In 1986, the Club purchased handicapping computer software for use in the golf pro shop. The tennis program was quite active during this decade. A new pro shop was added as well as the first Har-Tru courts. Additionally, a new tennis practice board was constructed on the old former maintenance shed concrete slab.

Top: *Alex McKechnie, Bob Nickey, and Foster Hopkins*

Bottom: *West Shore Christmas Talley 'n Tee, 1994*

The swimming pool was showing signs of age and, throughout the decade, there were various suggestions as to how best to deal with the problems. In 1981, it was recommended that a year-round pool facility be constructed. In spite of the difficulties with the pool, the West Shore swim team proved to be a dominant group and consistently placed at the top in the league championships.

Among the many regular social events at the Club were dinner-dances, Talley 'n Tees, various holiday picnics, bingo, and the Friday Night Supper Club. In addition to the social events, the 1980s saw many other actions taken by the Board of Governors: the approval of the conversion of the heating system from oil to gas in order to reduce costs; legal procedures to redeem all outstanding valid shares and certificates of capital stock; the institution of "cycle billing"; the rejection of the acquisition of land known as "Floribunda Heights" for an additional nine holes of golf; the enactment of the "Forever Green Project" under which ninety-five new trees were to be planted during the next four planting seasons; the establishment of a dress code for the Club; the rejection of a merger between the West Shore Country Club and the Harrisburg Country Club; and the elimination of all pull-carts.

Much was done over the years to improve the décor of the clubhouse and ongoing fiscal stewardship by the governors kept the Club relatively debt-free, which provided a managerial model for future endeavors.

But the years did take their toll and, besides the natural deterioration of an old building, the heating and cooling systems were a constant problem. Of major concern was that the air conditioning system might malfunction during one of those ninety-eight-degree days with more than 200 people in the ballroom. The Board carefully examined all the remodeling options but eventually reached the conclusion that the Club was facing a long-term problem that required more than a "band-aid," or short-term solution.

During the 1990s, when the World Wide Web was in its infancy, the West Shore Country Club was busy addressing those remodeling concerns, which became the focus of many, many Board meetings and committee discussions. By 1992, a questionnaire was sent out to each active member soliciting input on what and how many renovations should be undertaken by the Club. A total of 281 replies to the questionnaire were received and tabulated, the results forwarded to the architect who was hired to assess the future needs of the Club. From that was born the swimming pool project. A special meeting was called on June 14, 1993, and those in attendance voted overwhelmingly to approve the construction of a new pool, at a cost not to exceed $950,000. Once completed, the pool allowed the West Shore swim team to become much more competitive.

The West Shore gang prepares for another trip to Happy Valley. West Shore used to hold bus trips to PSU games in the 1970s and 1980s.

Pro shop and courtyard from first tee in 1999

The last vestiges of the "old" order were erased during this decade, when women were finally allowed equal access to all areas of the Club, and the health concerns of the membership were addressed by restricting tobacco use to designated areas on the grounds.

In 1998, President Lee Turner appointed Carlton Hughes and Bill Etzweiler as co-chairs of an ad hoc Building Committee. Previously, there had been a feasibility study for a new clubhouse, conducted by an outside consultant. There was a subsequent meeting of the membership where the vote was 132 to 32 to allocate funds for the employment of an architect. In January 1999, after reviewing the credentials of twenty-three architectural firms, Alexander Design/Chambers Company was retained to design and decorate the new clubhouse. Ralph Klinepeter, president of Pyramid Construction Services and a member of the West Shore Country Club, agreed to serve as the owner's representative during the upcoming construction. Preliminary designs were completed and there were a number of open informational meetings for the membership. On October 25, 1999, at a special membership meeting, the vote was 134 to 87 to proceed with the construction of a new clubhouse at a cost not to exceed $8.5 million.

ENTER A NEW MILLENNIUM

As the momentous year of 2000 appeared on the calendar, at the West Shore Country Club, the construction of a new $8.5-million clubhouse finally got underway after over five decades of: *Shall we do this?* The first action was relocating the golf pro shop to the ladies' lounge and club storage into the old clubhouse

corridor. Groundbreaking was in June. Because of years of silt collection in the pond at No. 13, it was dredged to increase its water-holding capacity. The existing $99,843 swimming pool mortgage was paid off in June 2000. A "demonstration project" for bunkers on No. 13 and No. 14 was completed in the fall of 2000 at a cost not to exceed $45,150. At the annual meeting in 2000, an "absentee balloting" by-law was adopted.

There were some issues that had to be resolved during the pre-construction and construction phases of the project. One that required immediate attention was discovery of an area best described as "oil-impacted" soil from a 1990s oil leakage, which had to be disposed of according to environmental specifications. The cost was $400,000. Another issue concerned retaining the old farmhouse as an entrance for the new clubhouse, something the architect recommended but which was rejected by the membership. Finally, after completion, Barclay-White Contractors turned over the keys to our new facility. In what was an almost seamless transition, the move from old to new quarters was carried out in two days with no interruption in service or Club activities—a rather remarkable management achievement. On May 4, 2002, there was a gala dinner-dance attracting 350 to what was an elegant black-tie event.

Top: *New Years Eve, 1995*

Middle: *Patti Seick, Barb and Merv Holland, Marty Knerr, and Clarence Burner enjoy a class reunion at West Shore in 1999.*

Bottom: *Party on the old patio in August 1999*

After a thorough study and no overwhelming interest in spending another million dollars to render usable the old clubhouse, it was demolished. Three town meetings attracted over one hundred members; at each scheduled session, two auctions of old clubhouse items brought in $25,000. A luncheon to recognize fifty-year members, in addition to adding their names to a wall plaque, was instituted in 2002. Additional rounds of golf

were accorded to persons on the Social and Retired lists. A grand opening black-tie dinner-dance was enjoyed by 350 guests on May 4, 2002. By that summer, a serious summer draught instituted restricted watering procedures.

A several-stage landscaping plan submitted by a committee chaired by Henry Line was implemented. A record 33,186 rounds of golf were recorded in 2002, and at the end of the year, there were seventy-eight persons on the transfer waiting list. In December 2002, Mr. Scott Irwin was offered the position of general manager to assume his duties in February 2003. President Arndt was named interim acting Club manager.

The year 2003 marked improvements to the existing Har-Tru tennis courts and play began on the new tennis courts. The Drummer Boy was selected as the official emblem of the West Shore Country Club. A new golf practice and driving range was constructed and opened. At the member-guest putting contest, a guest from Gettysburg holed a 120-foot slider on the new putting green to win $10,000. President Arndt continued the informative town meetings. A seventy-fifth anniversary celebration was held at the Club in 2003. The financial proposal for a

Top left: *To build a structure, first you dig a hole.*

Top right: *New clubhouse takes shape in 2000*

Bottom: *Demolition of old clubhouse with new structure in background, 2002*

seven-year fixed rate for the bunker project was 5.5 percent. The courtyard was named Bowman Terrace.

The food and beverage minimum was eliminated for retired members with over fifty years of continuous membership at the Club. Thirty persons were transferred from Active to Senior Active status in 2005. Gold tee markings for seniors were added to each tee. The Metzger Tennis Tournament was held at the Club for the first time. The *a la carte* gratuity was raised to 18 percent. A $352,000 plan was submitted to the House Committee to finish the house decorations. The Bunker Renovation Project was completed. A mailbox in memory of past treasurer Ralph Wire was located across the driveway from the main entrance to the Club.

In 2005, the USGA amateur qualifier was held at the Club in August. The creek on hole No. 12 was reopened. A beautiful ornamental iron fence along part of Brentwater Road was installed. A working relationship with a local health club was established. Record-setting heat was experienced in July and August. The Golfnet tee time service was authorized. More trees were removed under the Restoration Project. A master plan for professionally decorating the clubhouse was undertaken.

In 2006, a non-resident select membership was adopted. The selective tree removal program continued with 228 trees no longer "cluttering" the golf course. After forty years of faithful service and one last called number, a new bingo machine was purchased. A property replacement study was approved. A machine was purchased for the tennis complex. An innovative lighting project on the No. 1 hole brought nightly scenic beauty to diners in the Club restaurants. Two additional defibrillators were purchased and placed at the tennis courts and in the clubhouse. The tax assessment bill rose to $123,317. It was also noted that only 22,600 rounds of golf were played that year, the lowest number since 2002.

The budget for 2007 was approved for $2.7 million. A new Junior program of membership for those aged twenty-one to thirty-five was adopted and a new program for children of current members called Junior Legacy was added to the by-laws. A town meeting was convened in October for the purpose of explaining, detailing, and answering questions about the proposed "West Shore Country Club Capital Reserve Study" that was adopted at the annual meeting in November. The outstanding debt of the Club as it entered the 2007 fiscal year was $6,406,000. Finally, in

keeping with the times, a thorough non-smoking policy was adopted for West Shore Country Club. Oh, what the original founders would have said about that!

MOVING FORWARD—CLUBHOUSE UPGRADE CONCEPTS

When Barclay-White Contractors turned over the keys to our existing clubhouse facility, it did not mean that time would stand still and there would be no future changes.

In the seven years since the completion of the new clubhouse, there have been growing pains and great satisfaction. Several changes are under serious consideration and one may even be complete by the time this account is published.

First, renovations to the stage in the ballroom are needed. The stage area is rather drab and needs attention. Judd Brown Designs has been contracted and its concept for the ballroom stage is in the 2009 capital budget.

Secondly, a transformation of the Men's Card Room to a true "19th Hole" is under consideration. The Men's Card Room would be relocated to the current locker room. This new area would complement the new patio completed in 2008. It would create a casual grille to serve the course and locker rooms. A new bar and flat-screen TVs would be included along with liquor display and storage. Versatile seating in tables to seat four would make the room the perfect place to stop for a quick beverage or snack following golf or tennis.

Top left: The Hearth Room invites members and guests into a warm environment. Friday Happy Hour is a popular time in the Hearth Room.

Top right: The Overlook Room offers fine dining in a sophisticated atmosphere.

Bottom: Former New York City Mayor Rudy Giuliani meets the media on March 13, 2008, in West Shore's Hearth Room. Giuliani was in town to campaign for presidential candidate John McCain.

Opposite page, bottom left: Bob Nickey's pro shop has a varied selection of merchandise for golfers of all shapes and sizes.

Preliminary Clubhouse Interior Master Plan

Judd Brown's architectual renderings on this page show the conceptual changes to the ballroom, which likely will be completed in 2010 or shortly thereafter. The "19th Hole" is a project slated for the future.

That the West Shore Country Club is held in high esteem by its members is the principal reason for our enduring success. While this simple fact seems self-evident (if it were otherwise, why else would we

continue on as members?) less obvious is the degree of love that certain of our members have had for their Club. And because of it, West Shore is indeed blessed.

Very noteworthy in this regard is Ralph Wire, who served the Club so well for many years as its treasurer. As a memorial to that special relationship between Ralph and West Shore, his wife, Marge, and his children contributed the stone mailbox that so elegantly adorns the entrance to the Club.

Similarly, as explained in this book, George Hoopy enjoyed a very special relationship with West Shore—very special indeed! George was the only member in the Club's history for whom it can be said was born here, in 1906 in what was our old clubhouse. So it was that for these reasons, and, likely, many others more personal, Mr. Hoopy remembered West Shore in his will, the ultimate testimony of what West Shore meant to Mr. Hoopy. The monies from this remembrance have recently been received.

Prior to his passing, Mr. Hoopy inquired as to whether there might be any special need or project that the Club had that his

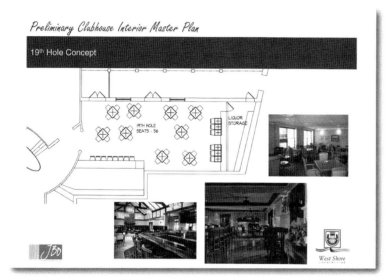

passing could make possible. He was informed of the Club's dire need for a stone staircase, so often a topic of discussion among the members and seemingly always outside the reach of the annual budgets, and which was indeed such a project. This recommendation was found satisfactory by George and little more was mentioned about it in this regard until the announcement of the bequest. Upon its receipt, the Board of Governors assigned to the Long Range Planning Committee the stewardship of the monies. The committee, with the endorsement of the Board, identified three key criteria which should be satisfied by any proposed project: the project must be long-lasting, it should be a project that can be enjoyed by all segments of the Club's membership, and it must be a noteworthy memorial to Mr. Hoopy. The staircase that had been discussed with him well satisfies all three criteria.

As a small token of appreciation for Mr. Hoopy's thoughtfulness, the Board of Governors unanimously approved the naming of the entranceway to the Club as Hoopy Lane and a sign so noting has been erected, reminding us all of how special a member George Hoopy truly was.

4

THE WEST SHORE
GOLF COURSE

True students of golf and golf courses can generally spot a golf course designed by a Donald Ross
or a Robert Trent Jones or a Pete Dye simply by
knowing the design philosophies that character-
ize the work of these great architects. Locally, the
Country Club of York is a Donald Ross layout.

Other famous golf course architects also practiced their handi-work in Central Pennsylvania: William Flynn—famous for Cherry Hills in Colorado; the Country Club of Brookline, Massachusetts; Philadelphia Country Club; and Lancaster Country Club—also designed the golf course for the Country Club of Harrisburg. Maurice McCarthy designed or re-modeled 125 courses in his life-time, but his most famous works are the four courses he designed in Hershey, including Hershey Country Club (West) and the Parkview course. Both Colonial Country Club and Blue Mountain Golf Club were designed by David Gordon of Philadelphia, while George Fazio designed Hershey Country Club (East) and Silver Spring Golf Course. All of these men rank among the most highly respected golf course architects in the world, which makes a strong statement about how seriously Central Pennsylvanians take their golf.

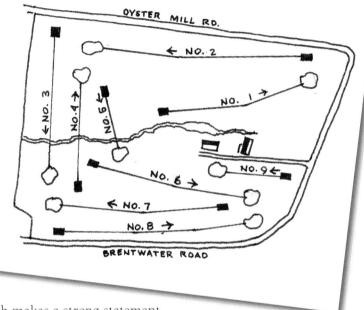

Drawing of the original nine-hole layout

Noticeably absent from this history of golf course architec-ture in Central Pennsylvania is the West Shore Country Club.

The design of West Shore's golf course has evolved over our history in four major phases: the original nine holes designed by George Morris, the second nine holes designed by M. E. Moyer and Jack Norrie, the revisions of the Ed Tabor era, and the Gil Hanse renovation. In 1928, shortly after the Club was organized, the original sixty-nine-acre Kiehl farm was purchased. The Board of Governors authorized the sum of $125 to be paid to then Colonial Country Club golf professional George Morris for the design plan for the original nine holes (current holes No. 1, 2, 7, 8, 9, 10, 11, 17, and 18).

That may not seem too impressive at first glance, but George Morris's great uncle, Old Tom Morris, is history's first profes-sional greenskeeper, as well as the premier golf course designer in all of Britain during the last half of the nineteenth century. Before retiring, he taught his craft to a young Scot named Donald Ross,

The No. 6 green looking back to the sixth fairway. This 1940s photo, probably taken during an exhibition in the 1940s, shows the rolling hills and farm-like nature of the property.

who went on to become the father of American golf course architecture. So, almost by accident, the original nine at West Shore Country Club had "blue blood" running through its veins. If genealogy can be transferred from men to golf holes, our "original nine" is a direct descendent of the "Old Course" of the Royal and Ancient, St. Andrews, Scotland!

George Morris's grandfather, also named George, was the brother of the legendary Old Tom Morris of St. Andrews, Scotland. His grandfather had designed the back nine at Royal Liverpool Golf Club, Hoylake, England, where he also had been the golf professional. He was succeeded as pro at Royal Liverpool by his son, Jack, whose son George emigrated to this country as a young man and became the golf professional at Colonial Country Club in 1922.

The first three holes (current holes No. 1, 2, and 9) were completed in 1929, and all the holes of the original nine were officially opened for play on May 3, 1930. Soon thereafter, proposals were floated to purchase the ninety-five acre Brinton farm adjoining the property to the north. However, the purchase of the adjoining farm was not consummated until June 1935. The Board then passed a resolution authorizing the Green Committee, together with golf professional Jack Norrie, to employ a golf architect to provide plans for the extension of the course at a cost not to exceed $200. However, a subsequent resolution to raise the dues from thirty-five dollars to fifty dollars to finance the project was defeated by vote of the membership at the 1935 annual meeting. The Board minutes are not entirely clear on the issue, but the resolution to spend $200 to hire a golf architect was apparently abandoned upon the defeat of the dues increase. Although he would have been the logical choice, there is no record in the minutes that George Morris was consulted or had any input into the design of the new nine holes.

At the February 1936 Board meeting, Mr. M. E. Moyer was appointed Green Committee chairman, and the minutes further state: "Mr. Moyer of the Greens Committee submitted a plan for the development of the additional nine holes on the Brinton Farm…. [D]evelopment was authorized according to the plan as funds permit." Mr. Moyer, who served as greens chairman until 1940, shares credit for the design of the second nine holes (current holes No. 3, 4, 5, 6, 12, 13, 14, 15, and 16) with Jack Norrie, the

golf professional/superinten-dent at the time, who is known to have supervised construction of the new nine, which was not completed until 1939. Both nines were laid out on treeless farmland, with rudimentary "push-up" greens and minimal movement of earth. Bunkers were few and far between. All of the original greens have subsequently been rebuilt, and most of the bunkers were added later, so that the only major feature of the original design that survives to this day is the routing of the golf holes through the property.

The next major phase took place under the direc-tion of longtime golf profes-sional/superintendent Ed Tabor, who, between 1944 and 1978, rebuilt every green on the golf course and expanded or added a total of sixty-two bunkers.

He is responsible for countless other improvements, but his most prominent contribution to the design of the golf course, as it exists today, is the marvelously designed greens. Although he had no formal training in golf course architecture, at his previous post at Wanango Country Club in Dubois, he worked alongside John Davidson, who had been a senior foreman for the famous golf

Top: *Pro Ed Tabor hits from the original No. 4 tee in the 1950s*

Bottom: *Old bunkering near the No. 12 green. Where is the creek?*

course architect Donald Ross. From this association and from his experiences as a PGA professional, he became an astute interpreter of the Donald Ross style, which he applied in his thoughtful redesign of our greens. Ed Tabor was a student of Dick Wilson, who also designed several of the famous Pinehurst courses. One of Ed's favorite courses was Wilmington Country Club, which he and his son Jim visited to study Wilson's architectural style.

Jim used that learning experience in putting his hand to the course in the 1960s and 1970s, redesigning the greens at No. 9, 11, 15, 16, and 18.

The final phase was the implementation in 2002–2004 of the Bunker Renovation Plan designed by up-and-coming golf course architect Gil Hanse, assisted by his design partner, Jim Wagner. The plan consisted of the complete re-bunkering of the golf course with a total of eighty-two bunkers, as well as the re-contouring of the fairways, the addition and relocation of forward tees, the removal of obtrusive trees, and the establishment of native grass areas. In his written evaluation of the design of the golf course, Mr. Hanse recognized that the routing and the greens were the strongest features and should not be disturbed:

The course layout works with the wonderful terrain in many impressive aspects. The topography with numerous

The beautiful ninth from the tee in spring

natural features allows the course to be skillfully routed and provides a solid framework for the golf course… [W]e feel the excellence of the greens are the backbone of the golf course… From the roller coaster ride of the first green, all the way to the last putt, these greens demand your attention and respect. For a course not designed by a "name" architect, these are perhaps some of the best greens.

The Bunker Renovation Plan was designed to build on the strength of the existing greens and routing, and produce a finished product in a style reminiscent of the great architects of the first half of the twentieth century that has come to be known as the "Golden Age" of golf course design. While his design for our golf course is his own unique artistic creation, Mr. Hanse's improvements have resulted in a traditional parkland golf course similar in style to the designs of William Flynn, A. W. Tillinghast, George Thomas, and others identified with "The Philadelphia School" of golf design.

Mr. Hanse received critical acclaim for both his original creations (e.g., Boston Golf Club, Rustic Canyon, and Applebrook) and his restorations of "Top 100" courses designed by the old masters (e.g., Fishers Island Club, Plainfield Country Club, Quaker Ridge Golf Club, Fenway Golf Club, The Kittansett Club, Ridgewood Country Club, and Sleepy Hollow Country Club). Often compared favorably with architects such as Tom Doak and Bill Coore & Ben Crenshaw, he is now world-renowned and critically acclaimed as one of the most gifted designers in the minimalist "Golden Age" style. Mr. Hanse has been retained on a continuing basis to guide the West Shore Country Club in the implementation of the multitude of "finishing touches" that are the mark of a well-designed golf course.

Top: *Gil Hanse*

Bottom: *Team of Gil Hanse Golf Design surveying the course prior to bunker renovations*

Amazingly enough, this hodgepodge of contributors, including a descendent of Old Tom Morris, an architect so noteworthy that no one can remember his name, a golf professional/superintendent and, later, an up-and-coming designer who would go on to draw up some great modern courses, collectively produced a genuine "sleeper" among the great golf courses in Pennsylvania, a course that constantly surprises first-time guests from other regions who "can't believe they've never heard of this course!"

Thomas Mitchell Morris, Sr. (June 16, 1821–May 24, 1908), otherwise known as Old Tom Morris, was one of the pioneers of professional golf. He was born in St. Andrews, Fife, Scotland, the "home of golf" and location of the St. Andrews Links, and died there as well. His son, Tom Morris, Jr. (d. 1875), best known as Young Tom Morris, was also a champion golfer.

Morris was an apprentice to Allan Robertson, generally regarded as the first professional golfer. He worked as a greenskeeper, clubmaker, and course designer, as well as playing tournament golf. He came in second in the first Open Championship in 1860, and won the following year. He followed this up with further victories in 1862, 1864, and 1867. He still holds records as the oldest winner of the Open Championship at forty-six. Also, he was part of the only father-son couple to be winner and runner-up.

WEST SHORE'S LINEAGE—OLD TOM MORRIS

Morris played a role in designing courses across the British Isles, including Muirfield, Prestwick, Carnoustie, Moray, Warkworth in Northumberland in the same year as Muirfield (1891), Askernish links in South Uist, and Rosapenna links in Ireland.

There is currently a road in St. Andrews, Fife, named after him. The eighteenth hole of St. Andrews golf course is also named after the golfer in memory of his commitment to the course, and to golf in general.

Tom Morris was also the father of modern greenskeeping. He introduced the concept of top-dressing greens and introduced many novel ideas on turf and course management, including actively managing hazards (in the past, bunkers and the like were largely left to their own devices, becoming truly hazardous). In course design, he standardized the golf course length at eighteen holes (St. Andrews had at one time been twenty-three holes), and introduced the concept of each nine holes returning to the clubhouse. He also introduced the modern idea of placing hazards so that the golf ball could be routed around them. Before his time, hazards were thought of as obstacles that either had to be carried or were there to punish a wayward ball.

5

THE TOUR OF
THE GOLF COURSE—THEN AND NOW

"The course layout works with the wonderful terrain in many impressive aspects. The topography with numerous natural features allows the course to be skillfully routed and provides a solid framework for the golf course…" This early description of the West Shore golf course holds true today. What follows is a hole-by-hole tour of the golf course with photos of the course as it was prior to the Hanse redesign and how it looks today.

Hole No. 1—*Another Tom Morris protégé, Donald Ross, stated that the first hole should be a "handshake hole" to introduce the player to the course. At 289 yards, West Shore's No. 1 fits this description. But don't go left, right, long, or short…*

Hole No. 2—*Gil Hanse's bunker redesign, in the spirit of Tom Morris, requires that the player steer around hazards on the tee shot and second shot of this par 5.*

Hole No. 3—*Tree removal behind the green has opened grand vistas of the rolling hills beyond. It also serves to challenge the player's distance control and depth perception.*

Hole No. 4—*Again, here at West Shore's number one handicap hole, the fairway bunkers challenge the player's accuracy to set up a short to medium iron shot into the green.*

Hole No. 5—*By moving the fairway bunker from the left to the right side, Hanse's redesign requires the player to overcome the natural slope of the land toward the bunker.*

Hole No. 6—*Removal of the right greenside bunker and the establishment of a collection area requires a deft short game should the player miss right. This style is reminiscent of Donald Ross's "crowned" or "turtleback" greens, most famously seen on Pinehurst No. 2.*

Hole No. 7—*One of the longer par 4s at West Shore, players must avoid the left fairway bunker off the tee or most likely have no chance of reaching the bunkerless green in regulation.*

Hole No. 8—*At 290 yards from the regular tee, the hole underwent a dramatic transformation with the removal of the left grove of pines and the construction of the fairway bunkering.*

Hole No. 10—*From the championship tee, this hole becomes demanding in that it requires a solid strike off the tee to set up a mid-iron to a well-protected green.*

Hole No. 11—*The prevailing westerly winds make this dogleg downhill hole play much longer than its 425 yards from the championship tee. It can be the "hardest par" on the course in some conditions. The green was one of only a couple that were rebuilt since their original construction and tweaks by Ed Tabor in the 1930s and 1940s.*

Left: **Hole No. 9**—*Originally, only a small stream fronted this green, as seen in this photo (inset) from an old competition. The green is now protected by a pond and pot bunkering on the right side.*

Hole No. 12—*Dramatic changes to the look of this hole included the fairway relocation and bunkering on the hill, along with the opening of the creek. Although short for a par 5, it requires the player to avoid both sand and water hazards, resulting in a three-shot hole for most.*

Hole No. 13—*The uphill tee shot some-times plays longer from the forward tees due to the elevation change.*

Hole No. 14—*A short tee shot can make the player have to choose a lay-up on the second short. The green beautifully tucked into a wooded area is surrounded by trouble.*

Hole No. 15—*Long hitters take aim to drive this short par 4. However, a wayward attempt usually results in a bogey or worse.*

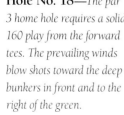

Hole No. 17—*Hanse's introduction of the cross fairway bunker at 145 yards from the green made the most dramatic impact of any on the golf course. The second shot on No. 17 is one of the most challenging on the golf course.*

Hole No. 18—*The par 3 home hole requires a solid 160 play from the forward tees. The prevailing winds blow shots toward the deep bunkers in front and to the right of the green.*

Right: **Hole No. 16**—*Often featured among the finest golf holes in Central Pennsylvania, the 438 hole from the championship tees requires a mid- to long iron into a heavily bunkered green.*

6

EIGHTY YEARS OF GOLF
AT THE WEST SHORE COUNTRY CLUB

Since its beginning as a nine-hole course in 1928 and through the fifty years of its growth, the West Shore Country Club golf course has proven to be a true test of golf to many of the finest players in Central Pennsylvania and, on numerous occasions, the world's finest. It is a tribute to the foresight and energy of those early members of this Club that such is the case. Working with limited budgets and developing the Club through the lean years of the Depression, it is a wonder that they survived at all.

It wasn't until 1932 that Jack Norrie was hired as a combination pro and greenskeeper, although a Mr. Lee was appointed caddy master in 1930. Greens fees were one dollar and fifty cents on weekends and one dollar on all other days. Golf balls were purchased wholesale from a local sporting goods store for fifty-five cents and sold to members for seventy-five cents. For many years, members contributed trees for planting on the course and actually performed the labor of planting them.

So, many years later, as we go through the process of removing many of these trees, we know who to blame! But this was the reason West Shore survived during these critical years—a cooperative sense of responsibility and a willingness to work toward success. In 1935, an offer to purchase the ninety-five-acre Brinton Farm for $10,000 was approved, and in about two years, the eighteen-hole course that we now know was completed.

In order to stimulate interest in golf and membership in the Club, numerous exhibitions have been staged over the years by some of the world's greatest golfers. And attesting to the challenge of our course is the fact that none of them has really "torn the course apart" with phenomenal scores. In 1930, Billy Burke and Joe Turnesa played an exhibition. In 1936, Alex Morrison and Henry Picard put on an exhibition and golf lesson. The ladies

September 14, 1946, "West Shore Country Club Teams Play Match." The men's golf team of the West Shore Country Club defeated the women's team 13 to 3 in a handicap tournament on the West Shore course.

Members of the teams relaxing before starting the match are John Weaver, Sr., W. W. Sponsier, Harold Miller, J. D. Johnson, Robert Shaw, Reid Bennett, Dr. P. J. Andrews, J. M. Robb, H. E. Mowery, Dr. John Lanshe, William Lampe, Herman Hain, Richard Reed, J. S. Williamson, Roland Knox, William Donges, Miss Ann Barnitz, Mrs. J. V. White, Mrs. E. A. Town, Mrs. J. D. Johnson, Mrs. J. A. Straits, Mrs. Donald Stouffer, Mrs. John Wismer, Miss Virginia Corkran, Mrs. George N. Wade, Mrs. Fred Wigfield, Jr., Mrs. C. W. Hull, Mrs. E. A. Groene, Mrs. R. M. Wachob, Mrs. E. M. Craighead, Mrs. M. F. Kime, and Mrs. John McKay.

Left: *West Shore Golf Pro Joe Davis in 1939.*

Right: *From left to right: Bob Helms, Sr., Mickey Lindenberger, and Fred Reeser. Kneeling is John Weaver, Sr.*

were thrilled when Patty Berg and Helen Detwiler played before a crowd of 350 persons. In 1940, Henry Picard and Harold Miller teamed up against Jack Helms and Willie Turnesa, who had been National Amateur Champ.

West Shore has had many excellent golfers who have proven themselves on other courses as well as at home. The first Men's Club champion was S. E. Moyer in 1929, and the first Women's Club champion was Mrs. J. A. Straits in 1936. On the men's side, John D. Weaver, Jr. won seven Club championships, and his father, John D. Weaver, Sr., captured six titles. An interesting note is that John Weaver, Jr. succeeded his father as Club champion in 1949.

The Ladies Eighteen Hole golfing group has been a strong presence from early on in Club history. There are many fond memories of the beginning days where all members, men and women alike, actually pulled weeds to add another nine to the course and women raised money with bake sales. The Club was so busy that if you didn't bring your calendar to set up couples' golf dates during the Ladies Spring Rally, you were out of luck for the season! Without mentioning names, there are those who took players under their

Middle, left: *The West Shore Country Club team, composed of, left to right, Mrs. Edward A. Town, Mrs. William Lewis, Mrs. Salon Rhode, Mrs. Fred McDonell, and Mrs. O. R. Beaver, captured the First Annual Women's Harrisburg Team Match at the Country Club of Harrisburg. Mrs. Lewis carded an 82, the lowest gross score of the tournament. Mrs. C. H. Konhaus, team captain, was not present when the picture was taken.*

Opposite page, top: *Photo taken during a famous match in 1940. Jack Helms shot 68, Willie Turnesa carded 72, Henry Picard shot 72, and Harold Miller shot 75.*

Opposite page, bottom: *Mickey Lindenberger, George Wade, Woody Musselman, and John Weaver, Sr. putt out on the No. 18 green. The original clubhouse is in the background.*

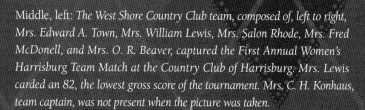

LADIES DAY WEST SHORE COUNTRY CLUB MAY 19, 1936

Hitting from the original first tee, the Championship tee

wing by teaching them to putt, a player who has thrown their clubs into the pond on No. 9, players who took charge, and players who are remembered fondly after their passing. It was often mentioned that quite a bit of attention was given by the community and the *Patriot News*. Tournament results were also announced at the monthly dinner-dances, which made the women feel like queens!

The first women's champion was Mrs. J. A. Straits in 1936. It is interesting to note that Mrs. Fran Konhaus has won the women's title a total of eight times, Mrs. Isabel Town a total of six times, and Mrs. Lorin W. High won five times. Another name mentioned often on the Championship Board is Rhea Singsen; she has won four times. She recalls one first-round match played against her opponent being determined by a phone call to the USGA by Bob Nickey for a ruling on their play on the thirteenth hole.

One name that appears on the Ladies Eighteen Hole Championship Board eleven times is Rusty Miller. Rusty has won many WSCC and district tournaments over the years and is proud to say that she broke 80 twice in her playing career. As written in the *Par Magazine* from 1978, "'Mother' Rusty won the Women's Golf Championship for the fifth time and then 'Dad' Earl and son Scott won the annual Father-Son Championship." Further down the road in 1988, a most memorable Women's Championship was recalled by Rusty. Her daughter, Carol Miller Dressel, bested her in an exciting eighteen-hole final while she was nine months pregnant. Stephen Colin Dressel was born shortly after and is now on the golf team at Elon University. Now that's a golfing family!

Opposite page: Ladies' Opening Day 2008 (top) and Opening Day May 13, 1936 (bottom)

In 2006, the Ladies Eighteen Hole Championship was open to all golfing lady members of the Club and was sponsored by the Club. That year, the champion was Diane McArdle. All past Ladies Eighteen Hole champions are recognized as WSCC Women's Club champions. The youngest player, at twenty years old, to win the Women's Club Championship was Michelle Gill in 2007, who also won again in 2008 and 2009.

The Ladies Eighteen Hole Championship was renamed the Challenge Cup in 2006 and its first winner was Amy Hempt. The Ladies Eighteen Hole group continues to have a strong membership, great camaraderie, and can be found on the course every Wednesday trying to best their scores on our ever-challenging course.

Contributed by *Harrisburg Magazine* with permission to edit and reprint. Authored by Scott Campbell and published October 2007.

It is July 25, 1959. A sizeable group of spectators has gathered on the West Shore Country Club golf course to witness an eighteen-hole exhibition sponsored by the Club and the Ladies' Auxiliary of the Osteopathic Hospital. Four professionals comprise the playing group. Local club pros Dick Sleichter of Gettysburg Country Club and West Shore's Ed Tabor join two native Pennsylvanians who

GOLFER PREVAILS OVER HANDICAP

happen to be nationally recognized touring pros. One is Honesdale's Art Wall, Jr., the newly minted Masters champion. The other is a hard-hitting phenom from Latrobe named Arnold Palmer, whose alleged 67 on that day is believed to be the Club record from the blue tees. Among those following the foursome is thirty-two-year-old John D. Weaver, Jr., a superb amateur player who has a special connection to Palmer. And as the round is concluding on the last hole, Palmer glimpses Weaver's familiar visage and approaches him. After studying his face for a moment, he asks, "Johnny, where the hell have you been?" Indeed.

The two first met in the PIAA Golf Championship at Penn State in May of 1945. Weaver, a Camp Hill High School senior, had just copped the District 3 title at Reading Country Club. Upon his arrival in State College, he learned of Palmer's prodigious length off the tee. "My brother, who was a Penn State grad, did some bar-hopping the night before the tournament started and heard of Arnold's reputation," says John. "My dad told me to forget about him, and hit good irons and putt well, which were my two strengths anyway." To be sure, Reading sportswriter Chet Hagan's

Robert Shaw, Jr. congratulates 1949 Club championship winner Johnny Weaver, Jr.

account of Weaver's earlier district victory began, "Lanky, smiling Johnny Weaver... sinking long putts with the careless ease of a pro..."

By the third and final round of the PIAA competition, Weaver and Palmer were tied for the lead at 151. Not particularly long off the tee, John's solid short game neutralized his playing partner's booming drives. A seminal point in the contest occurred on a front nine par 3. "My tee shot came to rest on the front left of the three-tiered green," remembers Weaver. "Arnold was over the green behind the pin in the rough. I putted up over two levels, into the apron and out, then into the cup for an improbable birdie." John smiles as he recalls Arnold's reaction. "He just lowered his head and shook it back and forth." Palmer's difficult pitch ended up on the second level, where he three-putted for double. "I gained three strokes on that one hole," says John. "Otherwise, we were pretty even the rest of the day."

And it was Weaver's day, as he captured the state title with a fifty-four-hole total of 223. Palmer, only a sophomore, finished seven strokes back in a tie for third. He would return to claim the championship for the next two years before going on to greater accomplishments. However, for Weaver, the next two years were anything but greener pastures.

As the Second World War continued in the Pacific, John sought a way to serve his country after graduation. He received an appointment to the Pennsylvania Maritime Academy from State Senator George Wade. Classes were conducted aboard the USS *Suliner*, moored in

Philadelphia. In the fall of 1946, Weaver went on a training cruise to Martinique. "One night, around midnight, I was returning to the ship with a drunken sailor whose job it was to run the winch that hoisted the boat up to the davits," explains Weaver. "He ran the winch too fast, and the boat slammed up against the davits. The aft cable snapped and when the boat fell, hanging only by its fore cable, my left leg was crushed between the boat's bow and the davit." In that one moment, Weaver's life was irrevocably changed. Although it did not register immediately, his goal of becoming a PGA touring pro was now beyond reach.

He was flown to Portsmouth, Virginia's Naval Hospital, where surgeons wanted to amputate the damaged limb. Weaver's parents nixed that idea, preferring to save the leg. To that end, he was admitted to Hahnemann Hospital in January 1947 and remained there until September. "I was unable to turn up my foot because the anterior tibial nerve was severed," explains John. "The surgeons were never able to locate it among the damaged tissue, so I had to wear a full leg brace from my hospital discharge until about 1959. After that, I wore a brace that came up only to my knee."

Weaver learned to live with his handicap and, with few exceptions, walked competitive rounds of golf. Occasional discomfort prompted the use of pain medication. But in recent years, a decades-old prognosis was fulfilled. "I was told by a surgeon years ago that my condition would be tolerable until I reached a certain age, and then I would start to have trouble," he says. And that trouble culminated in the amputation of his left leg above the knee on December 26, 2005.

Now eighty years old, the Lower Paxton Township resident declares that he never knew a time in his life when he was not swinging a golf club. "My dad gave me a cut-off six-iron, and I would swing and swing and swing that club. I rode my bike to the West Shore Country Club with clubs across the handlebars. There, I'd watch the pro, Jack Helms, giving lessons to members. Then, I'd go practice what I saw. He had my idea of a perfect swing, so I watched him carefully."

Weaver's father, John, Sr., was one of the original founders of West Shore and a gifted player, as well. "Dad was a great encourager," says John. "But, as a salesman, he was on the road a lot and didn't really teach me the game. I also learned much from Dutch Harrison, who was the Club pro for a few years."

A portend of things to come occurred in the summer of 1939 when, at the age of twelve, Weaver carded a 77 at Carlisle Country Club. "I was supposed to caddy for my dad in an inter-club match with Carlisle," he explains. "However, when one of our players failed to show, I was asked to take his place. Fortunately, I had my clubs along. It was the first time that I broke 80."

Like most high schools of that era, Camp Hill did not have a golf team. "I joined with Clarence Berner and Jack Blair to have a few informal matches with Hershey," recalls Weaver. His scholastic links achievements were largely unappreciated until commencement, when school board president Ernest Latham paused to formally acknowledge John's PIAA title when presenting his diploma.

After discharge from the service, Weaver enrolled at Penn State's Harrisburg Center in 1949. "The university conducted a tournament at the old Colonial Country Club for freshmen from centers across the state," he says. "Most of the contestants were aiming to be on the varsity team, so the competition was good. I was fortunate enough to win."

While visiting the West Shore pro shop in 1950, Dutch Harrison was surprised to learn that Weaver had not registered to play in the prestigious All-American Tournament at Tam O'Shanter Country Club in Niles, Illinois. The event was the creation of Chicago entrepreneur George S. May, and featured pro golf's largest purse with separate competitions for pros, amateurs, and women. Harrison had an entry form sent to Weaver, who was scratch at the time. Weaver remembers the experience as if it happened a few weeks ago. "At the tournament, players were announced on the first tee to the crowd. When it was my turn to hit, it was dead silent. My brace made this clunking noise and I had to release it to bend over in order to tee my ball. After I hit a draw to the perfect location on the fairway and started off the tee, my partners told me to look around. The whole crowd was getting up from their seats to follow us."

"I played well until the last hole," says Weaver, "where my approach from the rough just failed to clear a creek in front of the green. A triple bogey on that hole was the reason I missed the cut."

Weaver enjoyed considerable local success. He claimed the West Shore Country Club Championship in 1949, 1950, 1959, 1960, and 1966, as well as the Blue Mountain (now Felicita) title in 1980. A score of 66 in the 1952 Harrisburg District Qualifier is one of his career highlights.

In 1981, he published *Putting with a Crutch*, a booklet that analyzes and promotes his method for accuracy with the flat stick. Weaver has been married to Helena "Bootie" Barrett (CHHS Class of '46) for fifty-six years. They have four children and six grandchildren.

In his introduction to Weaver's putting article in *Player*, editor-in-chief Mark Belinsky wrote, "Listening to him tell his story in his pleasant, lighthearted way, I couldn't help but appreciate his fine disposition... People like John Weaver serve as a good reminder that we have to take what comes and make the best of it."

The current Men's Club champion is Scott Christie, who made 2008 his fourteenth title. Scott outplayed defending champion and former PGA touring professional Greg Lesher in an epic twenty-hole final. Both Christie and Lesher were under par for the day, which started in the morning with semi-final matches with Christie dispatching of Bob Latham and Lesher defeating multiple championship winner George Dimoff.

Christie has also qualified for the U.S. Amateur and won the prestigious Jake Gitlen Memorial Tournament. The week prior to the 2008 Club Championship, Lesher, 1988 U.S. Open Low Amateur prior to turning pro, added the Gitlen trophy to his mantle.

In 2006, Greg Lesher completed the "West Shore Slam" if you will, winning the John D. Weaver Stroke Play Championship, the Club Championship, and the Ed Tabor Individual with teammate Chris Gephart.

In 2004, Bill Stasiulatis became the only player to hold the Men's Championship and the Senior Men's Championship in the same year.

For the record, three Club presidents have succeeded in winning the Club Championship: J. A. Wickenhaver, H. B. Miller, and H. A. Johnson. Hank Johnson has the distinction of being the only one to win the championship while serving as president.

Other essential ingredients in the success of a golf course are the pros and greenskeepers, who are responsible for the day-to-day operations. As mentioned before, it was in 1932 that Jack Norrie was employed as a combination pro and greenskeeper. Jack guided the Club through the troubled Depression years, as well as through the initial growth of the nine-hole course and the

Pro shop staff in the mid-1970s: Bob Nickey, Ed Tabor, and Gordon Neely

Drue Fenton, Rusty Miller, and Bob Nickey in a Patriot News photo, 1982

PGA touring pro Kirk Triplett visited with pro Bob Nickey in the mid-1990s.

Jeff Gribb with Rick Gibson, now pro at Lancaster Country Club

expansion into eighteen holes. In 1938, Joe Davis, then Norrie's assistant, was elevated to head pro, while Norrie devoted himself to greenskeeping duties full-time. Both men left the Club in 1939, and were succeeded by Jack Helms, who remained until 1941. The war years of 1942 and 1943 saw Dutch Harrison and Charlie Wipperman operating the pro shop. In 1944, Ed Tabor came upon the scene and was West Shore's pro for thirty-six years. He was succeeded by current head pro Bob Nickey in 1979. Tabor and Wipperman served in the dual capacity of pro and greenskeeper until the 1960s, when Riley Heckert was employed as golf course superintendent and was followed by Mike Liska. The fruits of the labor of our current superintendent, Brendon Clark, are evident in the layout of the course and in the playability and appearance of our greens and fairways.

Ed Tabor shows a classic set-up as he prepares to tee off.

WEST SHORE'S PRO—ED TABOR

It was noted in a 1978 booklet chronicling the first fifty years of West Shore Country Club that "in 1944, Ed Tabor came upon the scene and has been with us since, completing his 35th year in 1978."

Ed Tabor was more than West Shore's golf professional. His hand left an indelible mark on the golf course that will last for decades. He also left lasting impressions on many members—particularly youngsters, many who have grown to appreciate the game because of their time with Mr. Tabor.

For thirty-five years, Tabor served as golf professional, doubling as course superintendent for many years. He built or rebuilt many of the greens. Designer Gil Hanse left most of his work intact during the renovations in the mid-2000s. Tabor would often travel to different courses to study the work of great golf architects like Dick Wilson, Robert Trent Jones, Sr., and Donald Ross.

Ed Tabor, circa 1950

As a golfer, the best part of Tabor's game was putting and the short game. He had several LPGA tour players and others come to him for help with their game. Many of his amateur students were great short game players. He had a great rapport with young players. Junior Golf was one of his highest priorities.

In 1976, Tabor was recognized as Philadelphia Section PGA Professional of the Year. In 1978, West Shore created its men's district better ball tournament, which bears Ed Tabor's name today.

What is the Course Record?

According to history, during the war years (1942), Dutch Harrison, who was then the Club pro, played a match with Lloyd Mangrum, Jack Grout, and a Mr. Coffey from Baltimore. During this match, Harrison equaled the course record of 66, which had been posted by Jack Helms in 1940. The previous record of 68 had been set by Sid Wickenhaver and Joe Davis in the late 1930s. Since that time, the record has been tied in a competitive match by

Top: *A group of West Shore members accompanied Ed Tabor to the Greenbrier in the early 1980s to visit with Ed's longtime friend, Sam Sneed.*

Bottom: *Teaching Juniors was one of Ed Tabor's priorities.*

Johnny Weaver, Jr., while qualifying for the district championship in 1952. And, of course, some still recall the 67 by Arnold Palmer in 1959. More recently, Bill Kribbs shot 67 from the back tees while playing with pro Bob Nickey, and Hank Seidel carded a 64 from the white tees on a weekend outing with his dad. All of these scores are exceptional when we consider that many premier golfers have tested the course. Qualifiers for the National Open have been held here several times. District and state championships have been a part of our golfing program.

LPGA Hall of Famer Nancy Lopez and former husband Tim Melton (a local CBS sportscaster) offer congratulations during Ed Tabor Recognition Day. WSCC President Bill Kirchhoff (left) looks on.

George Bloom watches Governor Bill Scranton sign the Golf Week proclamation along with Senator George Wade (standing) and Ed Tabor.

Above: Ed Tabor presents the Tabor Championship trophy to Jeff Clements and Ed Short.

Right: Mr. Tabor was always a dapper dresser.

Hershey Country Club pro Charlie Gilbert, Governor Raymond Shaffer, Arnold Palmer, and Ed Tabor. Some remember that Charlie out-drove Palmer more than once that day.

Unfortunately, we have no definitive proof of the low round at West Shore in a USGA-sanctioned, hole-all-putts event. So, the "official" record is still there for the taking.

During recent years, the Tabor Tournaments have attracted the area's finest. Back in 1977, Rick Hrip and Charles Stringfellow posted a best-ball score of 63 in the Tabor Tournament, which was a record for better ball competition.

The "King" at West Shore

As noted previously, Arnold Palmer has had several connections with West Shore Country Club, and played at least two matches there that are recorded in history. In 1959, Palmer visited the Club and shot a 67—what is regarded as the unofficial course record from the championship tees. In 1970, he

Arnold Palmer tees off No. 1 at West Shore

played an exhibition match at West Shore that was staged by the Camp Hill High School Band Boosters to raise money for the band's Orange Bowl Parade appearance the following January. Governor Ray Shafer, Ed Tabor, and Hershey pro Charlie Gilbert played along with Palmer. Hundreds gathered to watch golf's "king" stroll West Shore's fairways and greens.

Top: *Palmer takes a familiar knocked-kneed putting stance on No. 6.*

Bottom: *A crowd surrounds the No. 3 green during the match.*

JUNIOR GOLF

Junior Golf at the West Shore Country Club has been and continues to be an important tradition. Junior Golf is the future of the game and the Club, for that matter. Longtime pro Ed Tabor established Junior Golf at West Shore. When, in 1976, Tabor was named PGA Professional of the Year by the Philadelphia Golf Association, among his many accomplishments was his Junior program.

Tabor taught countless children not only to enjoy the game, but to respect it as well. He had many successful students who went on to succeed in high school and college golf, as well as in the highest of amateur circuits. Several of his students went on to become West Shore Country Club champions, including Pete Delone, Scott Christie, Lee Turner, and Rick Gibson. More recently, Steve Buzby competed in the finals two years in a row, at ages fifteen and sixteen. You might be able to recognize some current members in the photos of "Mr. Tabor" with the Juniors.

Today, Bob Nickey's programs have been a big success. Like his mentor, Tabor, Nickey has been a promoter of Junior Golf for all the young boys and girls at the Club. Bob Nickey and Todd Love continue to draw large crowds for the group lessons and camps. There has been significant growth recently in lessons and play, according to Nickey.

West Shore's more recent Juniors have competed throughout the state successfully. Matt Plummer has qualified for several

Trophies for all in Mr. Tabor's Junior program in this 1970s photo.

AJGA tournaments. These are the highest-level tournaments in the U.S. for Juniors. His school, Cumberland Valley, is undefeated in high school competition. Quint Seidel has won the Harrisburg championships at Rich Valley and came in second in two other events. Jesse Hazam has been named Player of the Year for the NCPGA thirteen-to-fifteen age group. He did this as a thirteen-year-old, winning five times and coming in second on three occasions. There has also been a nice turnout for the parent-child golf tournament over the years. There is now consideration being given to establishing some kind of fun activity one Sunday evening a month, mixing kids and adults in some way.

Caddies at West Shore

The other aspect of Junior Golf at West Shore was the caddy program that was essentially terminated in the 1980s. Ed Tabor ran one of the best caddy programs in the Harrisburg area for nearly three decades. Many local kids, who otherwise would have no introduction to golf, were able to learn the game from one of the best. In addition, they had an advantage their parents did not: the chance to play golf once a week (every Monday morning) at West Shore Country Club.

7

TENNIS, ANYONE?

Tennis at the West Shore Country Club had a slow start when the Club was formed in April 1928, mostly because the founding fathers were avid golfers who made golfing their principal interest. However, there were two tennis courts authorized at $221 and the first tennis tournament was held in August of that year, with tennis balls awarded to the winners as prizes—at a cost of twelve dollars. The courts were used infrequently by members; weekend guests were allowed in for a seventy-five-cent fee that was subsequently reduced to fifty cents, then thirty-five cents during the Depression years.

Eventually, the courts gave way to the overwhelming desire by members for a swimming pool, which was later repaved for a parking lot. But then, interest in tennis started gaining momentum, especially following national and international play by Dwight F. Davis (for whom the Davis Cup is named), Bill Tilden, and Don Bridge. Again, two courts were built in another area, but they, too, were largely neglected during the World War II years. Then tennis interest was again revived when the Board of Governors created two new Club classifications, Social and Junior, with use of the courts as part of those membership privileges. Although there was more interest in golf, swimming, and bowling, tennis participation grew slowly, but steadily, and four modern courts were constructed. The cost was $24,000 and a tennis clubhouse replaced the former golf pro shop. Tennis was on the move and guests were welcomed at a two-dollar fee on weekdays and three dollars on weekends and holidays.

Tennis meetings were held monthly by non-playing Board members acting as chairmen. The courts were kept in good repair and the equipment was updated, such as ball machines, nets, the clubhouse, and surrounding shrubbery. The Board offered much support in the hiring of tennis pros. During 1975, a severe windstorm caused $17,000 worth of damage to the entire tennis complex, which also suffered ongoing damage by muskrats, groundhogs, and shrews. There were frequent discussions to erect a bubble over the courts for year-round play, but

Tennis at West Shore is a family affair, as this late 1990s photo shows.

those plans never materialized, perhaps because the cost was estimated to be $150,000 in addition to the salary for a year-round pro, electricity, and the cost of fence removal.

When the walkway to the tennis courts divided them from the pond area, one unsuspecting lady tennis player, on her way to the courts, was attacked by a male duck who was protecting his mate. The mother bird sat calmly on her nest warming her eggs, observing her mate cackling, wide-mouthed, with wings flapping, as he scared the astounded tennis player into the bushes. The tennis player made several attempts to escape him before finally sneaking away; fortunately, there was a round-about way to depart, avoiding his fury. And then there were two doubles players—one was six feet and four inches tall, and the other almost five feet tall. Prior to playing a match, the smaller fellow suggested to his partner, "You reach up and stop what you can, playing close to the net, and I'll run like heck at the base line and pick up on the long balls!" It was an effective and humorous strategy, and offered entertainment to the spectators.

Donna Saxon, Dawn Gribb, Jeff Gribb, and Joe Saxon relax after the matches during the 1989 Tennis Party.

In March 1976, Dr. Robert Morrison, a member of the Blue Ridge Country Club, arranged a meeting in his home for the purpose of setting up a tennis league with the other local country clubs—Colonial Country Club, the Country Club of Harrisburg, Hershey Country Club, and West Shore Country Club. Chuck Fromer and Donna Saxon represented West Shore Country Club. The league involved three categories: men's and women's singles and doubles, and Juniors (ages eighteen and under). Matches were held April through July with a final tournament and dinner party, at which time awards were presented to winners. Within a few years, York Outdoor, Allenberry, and York Country Club joined the group. These inter-club matches continue to the present.

Throughout the seventies to the present day, we have enjoyed an active member interest in the sport. Al Coons set up a Sunday

morning men's group. There was a Wednesday evening working women's group followed by dinner. The pros promoted round robins, monthly social parties, and Wimbledon parties in July featuring special English appetizers and the Wimbledon coverage of the final matches. A challenge ladder was supervised by Dr. Joe Savastio. The men's group was headed by Chuck Fromer, the ladies' group by Barb Nelson, and the Juniors by Pat Schmidt. During all this time, the clubhouse was updated and regularly stocked with clothing, racquets, balls, a machine for stringing racquets, and court and indoor and outdoor improvements. The Club was recognized as having the best tennis facilities in the area.

For many years, colorful circulars were mailed inviting players to "A Courtly Night," "Tennis Anyone," and "Match Power." The Tuesday night men's doubles were awarded Mickey Mouse T-shirts. In the late nineties, special attention was given to the Junior program. It was divided into age groups of four- to six-year-olds through eleven- to sixteen-year-olds. A Junior party/cook-out was enjoyed by thirty to forty Junior players. Interest by the pros has made this a popular category.

In 1987, the West Shore Country Club was the host for the first Hospice Tennis Classic in the area. Grace and Jim Robertson, avid tennis players, chaired this special event for several years. It has become an annual project involving other area tennis country clubs, and continues to support Hospice of Central PA.

The Metzger Tennis Tournament is another annual weekend event involving other local country clubs. It begins at West Shore Country Club on a Friday evening as part of the William H. Metzger Pennsylvania State Clay Court Open Championships.

Left: *Al Marks, Merv Holland, and Russ Knerr*

Right: *Tennis Party, late 1980s*

Russ Wileman gets ready to play.

Special pros, such as Luke Jensen, Tim Wilkinson, and Jimmy Aires play exciting matches, and then invite Club members for a fun clinic. The matches continue throughout the weekend at nearby country clubs. The Cystic Fibrosis Foundation of Central Pennsylvania benefits from their special weekend of tennis.

Several times we became involved with bus trips to the New York Open at Flushing Meadows, New York. Occasionally an overnight at a New York hotel was arranged. It was exciting to see premier players such as Ivan Mendl and Hannah Mendicova. On one memorable trip, we saw Pete Sampras defeat Andre Agassi and then watched the expertise of Steffe Graff, the lady's singles champion at that time.

Tennis at the West Shore Country Club has become an important part of Club life and the present courts are considered to be among the best in the area. From that slow start eighty years ago, tennis at West Shore Country Club is now an exciting part of Club life with a full schedule of lessons, matches, intra-Club and inter-club play, and tournaments along with a variety of social occasions that make tennis activity a vibrant value added to Club membership.

Top: *Ladies' group, 1999*

Middle: *Mixed competition is fun.*

Bottom: *Tennis professional Luke Jensen, West Shore pro Kevin Scott, Doris Wood, Sylvia Miller, and Donna Saxon*

8

WEST SHORE COUNTRY CLUB/
HOSPICE OF CENTRAL PA PARTNERSHIP

The twenty-eight-year-old relationship between the West Shore Country Club and Hospice of Central PA started in 1982, when two members of the West Shore Country Club approached the Board at the Club, asking if the fledgling organization, Hospice of Central PA, could do a small fundraising event at the country club. Bobbi Smith, who was a member of the Board of Directors of Hospice, and Jim Twigg, who also supported the organization, felt that a golf tournament would help to provide the three-year-old hospice organization with some operational money to help it "survive" and continue to provide services. Although the hospice concept was relatively unknown, the members of the West Shore Country Club Board generously agreed to host the event.

In June of that year, the first Hospice of Central PA Golf Tournament was held. Ladies played golf in the morning, and men played in the afternoon. An incredible total of $16,775 was raised as a result of this better-ball tournament. There were eighty-two ladies in the 8:30 a.m. tee-off and eighty men took part in the 2 p.m. tee-off. In addition to the players, thirty-one underwriting sponsorships were obtained.

In 1985, Jimmy Twigg turned the chairmanship of the event over to Jim Grandon. At the end of that year, the sponsorships had grown to fifty, and the event raised $23,845. By 1987, sponsorships grew to $84,000 under Jim Grandon's leadership.

In 1987, Elmer Reichwald, a newly retired ex-president of the Club, took over the chairmanship of the event. Because there had been a full field (128 men) playing in the golf event in 1986 and a waiting list, Reichwald and the committee went back to the Board of

Dr. Donald Friedman, West Shore pro Bob Nickey, Ms. Bobbi Smith, and Mr. Jim Twigg (shown here in 1982) were driving forces behind the success of the Hospice Tournament.

the West Shore Country Club and asked for an additional day on the course to help accommodate the growth of the extremely popular men's event. This request was granted and the men's and ladies' golf events were held on different days from 1987 forward. In 1987, Reichwald added the Ladies' and Men's Tennis Classics under the leadership of Grace and Jim Robertson. The Men's Tennis Classic was held on the same day as the Men's Golf Classic, allowing the participants to intermingle before play and at dinner. The event was renamed the Hospice of Central PA Golf and Tennis Classic to reflect the additional participation.

In 1988, Penn National Race Course started a new event, their Celebrity Jockey Race, which provided publicity for the golf tournament. That year, 120 sponsors raised $120,153 as part of the Golf and Tennis Classic.

The tournament with its four events continued to grow under the leadership of Elmer Reichwald. Men's golf was organized in a semi-competitive format with several "teams" of two trying to raise the most money. Competition was stiff but fun as committee members were trying not only to raise thousands of dollars each, but also to win a coveted gift certificate for fifty dollars at the pro shop.

Bob Nickey played a central role in both the ladies' and men's golf tournaments, sponsoring closest-to-the-pin contests, organizing the event, providing sponsor benefit packages, arranging each day's events, and making sure that things ran smoothly. The early tournaments were played out of a pro shop located in a separate building; it was later demolished as part of a renovation, and a new pro shop with greater capacity helped the Golf and Tennis Classic to expand. Bob Nickey received assistance from his wife, Annette, and his staff, especially Todd Love; both of them helped to play host to this event. Elmer Reichwald maintained the chairmanship of these events until he "retired" in 1994 and turned the leadership over to West Shore Country Club members Ralph Klinepeter and Ron Scott.

Contests that were held as part of the tournament started out with several of the local car dealers loaning cars for the day for a hole-in-one on hole No. 9. Although there were no hole-in-one winners, Jim Royer, also a member, offered a used car for several years to the person who was closest to the pin. Several out-bound college students were very appreciative of this. Currently, Hospice partners with Lexus Champions for Charity for both a hole-in-one car and a trip to their prestigious tournament courtesy of Bobby Rahal Lexus.

The photographer du jour since the event's inception has been Bill Mecaughey, a resident of Camp Hill and a professional photographer. Mecaughey volunteered to

Ms. Patty Latham and Ms. Marty Wileman were the winners of the 1984 Hospice Tournament.

do the photographs and has continued that very kind service since 1982. All of the photos for the first fifteen years of the event were in classic black and white. From year sixteen to year twenty-three, they were in color, and, since then, the photos have been captured in digital mode.

Mike May played a significant role in the success of the tournament by keeping the course in perfect shape each year for the tournament. As the first event of the Club's year, May and his staff worked in early spring to make sure that by the third Monday in the month of May, the course was ready for the event. Because spring is so beautiful on the course, the participants in the event spoke many times about their fortune in playing such a beautiful course.

By 1991, the Men's Hospice Golf Classic overflowed with over 264 players. Some men played at another course that year, but felt that they did not have the camaraderie that was shared at the West Shore Country Club. For future events, the maximum number of players was limited to 264, on a first-come-first-served basis, except in 2007, when several foursomes agreed to play at a different course and returned to West Shore Country Club for the evening banquet.

Top: *Diane Kohr and Maggie Wire welcome players to the Hospice Tournament.*

During the same time, the Ladies' Golf Tournament has also grown and had a full field of 128 players. On occasion, an extra foursome was added, but 128 was the official maximum. The ladies' event had its own chairs (or co-chairs), all from

Hospice of Central PA Headquarters has received funding from the West Shore Hospice Tournament.

the West Shore Country Club membership. It also did its own fundraising. Rather than emphasizing sponsorships that included players, the ladies' event concentrated on getting eighteen hole sponsorships each year. The ladies' golf event became well known as one of the most generous to its players in terms of sponsor packets and Ruby Romano started a tradition of obtaining the most unique and sought-after items to be part of the packet for each lady as a thank-you for playing.

As a small tribute of thanks to the West Shore Country Club, Hospice of Central PA provided a small garden at the eighteenth tee in 1991 to mark the tenth anniversary of the Golf Classic. After the clubhouse was rebuilt, several men who were members also made contributions, which provided a garden around the new clock bearing a sign denoting Hospice's gratitude to the West Shore Country Club members.

The Club management and staff provided support and guidance on a yearly basis for the Golf and Tennis Classic. Everyone on the staff from the manager to the kitchen crew was flexible, creative, generous, and accommodating. Those who came from other clubs to play in the tournament all felt a very welcoming atmosphere at the West Shore Country Club.

In 1998, Terry Luft joined the Men's Golf Committee. He became a co-chair in 1999, along with Doug Gibson, and from 2001 until 2005, he continued to co-chair the event with Harry Warren. Together, these teams brought a breadth of new supporters into the event along with new activities to keep the tournament appealing to those who attended.

In 2006, the twenty-fifth anniversary of the Golf and Tennis Classic was held with a special celebration to mark the event: a champagne toast, silver circles on the greens, the use of "twenty-five" as the theme for all prizes, and a special "longest drive" contest. For this event, Nelson Swarts took the chair, succeeding Harry Warren and Terry Luft, who had co-chaired the event for several years.

Over the years, the following members were chairs of the Men's Golf Tournament: Dale Bair, John Bolger, Doug Gibson, Jim Grandon, Jerry Hall, Ralph Klinepeter, A. L. Marks, Elmer Reichwald, Ron Scott, Rick Scott, Jim Twigg, and Harry Warren. This does not include the numerous individuals who also served on the Men's Golf Committee.

The new residents' facilities partially funded by West Shore's fundraiser have helped countless families in difficult times.

The Ladies' Golf Tournament was chaired by the following members: Sue Abbe, Mary Ann Adonizio, Gloria Basehore, Lynn Freitas, Jean Grandon, Sally Killian, Kim Klinepeter, Diane Kollas, Diane Kohr, Marri Lamoureaux, Evy Leo, Jane Miller, Mary Nissley, Barbara Patterson, Mary Eleanor Patterson, Nadine Penwell, Barbara Sherwood, Bobbi Smith, Bev Spatz, and Marty Wileman.

Funds raised through the generosity of this tournament through 2008 totaled over $3,000,000 (net). This allowed Hospice of Central PA to provide care to over 200 individuals and their families prior to any insurance benefits for hospice care. It continues to help cover many pain and symptom management medications for people whose insurance is capped or who have no hospice benefits.

These funds allow the agency to provide an extensive bereavement program to the community consisting of support groups, phone and written contacts, social groups, retreat weekends for grievers, a children's bereavement camp, and many other support activities. It also provides the agency with support to help reach out and provide extensive training to over 300 volunteers who provide family support, bereavement care, and administrative assistance. It also gave the agency the ability to open the only hospice house in the community and the second one in Pennsylvania.

9

WEST SHORE COUNTRY CLUB

SWIM TEAM

Over the years, the West Shore swim team has been a source of physical and emotional growth for the children of the country club members. Looking at some of the team photos from the 1970s (page 39), a careful eye can spot many current active members. After its formation, the swim team enjoyed decades of dominance due to the efforts of Bob Hughes, who formed a competitive team by introducing an inter-club league. Only when Rusty Owens became coach of the Colonial Park swim team did West Shore finally meet its match, producing a long-term, spirited, competitive environment between the two clubs.

Dreaming of a Perfect Season…

Like others before, the West Shore Sharks' 2008 summer season was a huge success as we finished the season with a record of five wins and one loss. Members agree that Coach John Butler, Coach Mike, Coach Suzy, and Coach Nellie have something special going for them. They create an atmosphere that inspires our kids to work hard to learn all of the strokes needed to compete while having fun at the same time.

West Shore Country Club is also fortunate to have PIAA State Champion and U.S. team member Leah Gingrich's spirit and experience as an assistant coach. Along with two state gold medals in 2008, Leah placed eighth in the U.S. Olympics swimming trials in the 800-meter freestyle in Omaha. The experience she gained over that week is something she will remember for years to come and use when the swimming trials roll around again for the 2012 Olympics in London, England. "It's been a wonderful time," Gingrich said thirty minutes after swimming the 800 free. "I'm so glad I got to experience this, because there is no other way to learn what the Olympics trials are like."

Top left: *Mini-team gets the little ones involved at early age.*

Top right: *The team celebrates another victory with Coach John.*

Bottom left: *Friendships develop on the West Shore swim team.*

Bottom right: *The girls show their medals.*

Coach John Butler—who, incidentally, before he was eight years old, was instructed in swimming at the YMCA by fellow coach Nelson Swarts—says, "In the five years I have had the pleasure of coaching this team, we have done nothing but improve." Butler believes the team's powerhouse comes from the fact no other team of swimmers has a greater parent base, or a greater sense of family, than the West Shore Country Club Sharks. Coach Nellie is not surprised by his commitment and his optimism. "It was obvious, even as a child, that Coach John could give and receive instruction well." In his first year as a coach for the Sharks, the team posted an even three wins to three losses, and the second and third year boasted four wins and two losses. The fourth and fifth years, 2007 and 2008, the Sharks declared five wins and one loss—quite a record to beat in 2009.

THE FUTURE OF WEST SHORE COUNTRY CLUB

For eighty years, the West Shore Country Club has enjoyed a reputation as a great place to enjoy friends and good times. Much of this is due to the family-friendly atmosphere and concentration on the development of our youngsters through many activities at the Club.

From Brunch with Santa to the Family New Year's Eve Party, "Dive in Movies," and Junior Golf programs, there is a special emphasis on youth development.

Over the years, many families have stayed with the Club through two, three, and sometimes four generations. Names include Jordan, Hempt, Latham, Tabor, Cleveland, Kirchhoff, Patterson,

Delone, Hughes, Christie, Green, Walters, Reilly, Kessler, and Seidel, along with others. Our apologies to anyone we have missed.

Recently, the Board of Governors approved a Legacy membership category to encourage young adults striking out after college to stay as members of West Shore as their careers and families develop.

This next generation and future generations will be the legacy that was started by Franklin Davies and the others in a different time.

SOCIAL EVENTS ABOUND

West Shore offers a wide variety of social events every year from the Christmas Formal, our most popular event, to the Texas Bar-B-Que and anywhere in between. The Club has been and continues to be the place for fun and entertaining evenings and events for adults and, in many cases, for the whole family.

CHAPTER TEN: SOCIAL EVENTS ABOUND | 133

Tournament Winners

MEN'S GOLF CHAMPIONS

1929	Samuel E. Moyer
1930	John A. Wickenhaver
1931	John D. Weaver
1932	Robert B. Kilborn
1933	John D. Weaver
1934	John D. Weaver
1935	Robert B. Kilborn
1936	William C. McEntee
1937	William C. McEntee
1938	Harold B. Miller
1939	Sidney L. Wickenhaver
1940	Harold B. Miller
1941	John D. Weaver
1942	Harold B. Miller
1943	Charles B. Fishel
1944	Harold B. Miller
1945	John D. Weaver
1946	Harold B. Miller
1947	Dr. P. T. Andrews
1948	John D. Weaver
1949	John D. Weaver, Jr.
1950	John D. Weaver, Jr.
1951	Robert C. Shaw, Jr.
1952	Robert C. Shaw, Jr.
1953	Lawrence N. Yost
1954	Robert C. Shaw, Jr.
1955	John D. Weaver
1956	Dr. P. T. Andrews
1957	John D. Weaver
1958	Robert C. Shaw, Jr.
1959	John D. Weaver, Jr.
1960	John D. Weaver, Jr.
1961	George R. Markley
1962	David P. Bruce
1963	David P. Bruce
1964	David P. Bruce
1965	Robert G. Wrightstone
1966	John D. Weaver, Jr.
1967	Thomas W. Markley
1968	Robert G. Wrightstone
1969	James E. Tabor
1970	James E. Tabor
1971	Robert G. Wrightstone
1972	James E. Tabor
1973	Clark K. Stecher
1974	Horace A. Johnson
1975	James E. Tabor
1976	Horace A. Johnson
1977	James E. Tabor
1978	Peter DeLone
1979	Peter DeLone
1980	Peter DeLone
1981	Lee C. Turner
1982	R. Scott Christie
1983	Horace A. Johnson
1984	R. Scott Christie
1985	R. Scott Christie
1986	R. Scott Christie
1987	Richard Gibson II
1988	R. Scott Christie
1989	R. Scott Christie
1990	R. Scott Christie
1991	William J. Kribbs
1992	R. Scott Christie
1993	R. Scott Christie
1994	R. Scott Christie
1995	R. Scott Christie
1996	George Dimoff
1997	R. Scott Christie
1998	Harry Warren III
1999	Harry Warren III
2000	Harry Warren III
2001	R. Scott Christie
2002	R. Scott Christie
2003	Bill Stasiulatis
2004	George Dimoff
2005	George Dimoff
2006	Greg Lesher
2007	Greg Lesher
2008	R. Scott Christie

WOMEN'S GOLF CHAMPIONS

1936	Mrs. Joseph A. Straits
1937	Mrs. Lorin W. High
1938	Mrs. Joseph A. Straits
1939	Mrs. Lorin W. High
1940	Mrs. Lorin W. High
1941	Mrs. Lorin W. High
1942	Mrs. Lorin W. High

1943	Mrs. Edward A. Town	1992	Rhea Singsen
1944	Mrs. Henry Picard	1993	Mrs. Gloria Basehore
1945	Mrs. Donald B. Stouffer	1994	Rhea Singsen
1946	Ann Barnitz	1995	Rhea Singsen
1947	Mrs. J. D. Johnson	1996	Caryn Rohrbaugh
1948	Ann Barnitz	1997	Caryn Rohrbaugh
1949	Ann Barnitz	1998	Caryn Rohrbaugh
1950	Mrs. Edward A. Town	1999	Mrs. Gloria Basehore
1951	Mrs. Edward A. Town	2000	Rusty Miller
1952	Mrs. J. D. Johnson	2001	Phyllis "Phyl" Mowery
1953	Mrs. Edward A. Town	2002	Amy Hempt
1954	Mrs. Fred Wigfield	2003	Kim Herbst
1955	Mrs. Donald B. Stouffer	2004	Rhea Singsen
1956	Mrs. Edward A. Town	2005	Amy Hempt
1957	Mrs. Elmer A. Groene	2006	Diane McArdle
1958	Mrs. Edward A. Town	2007	Michelle Gill
1959	Mrs. Carol H. Konhaus	2008	Michelle Gill
1960	Mrs. O. R. Beaver		
1961	Mrs. William L. Lewis		

BOB NICKEY OPEN WINNERS

2005	Hank Seidel	Doug Baillie
2006	Greg Johans	Bill Greenlee
2007	Art Campbell	Todd Love
2008	Doug Baillie	Jim Stubbs

1962	Mrs. William L. Lewis
1963	Mrs. Carol H. Konhaus
1964	Mrs. Carol H. Konhaus
1965	Mrs. Carol H. Konhaus
1966	Mrs. Charles E. Galley
1967	Mrs. Kenneth R. Stark, Jr.
1968	Mrs. Carol H. Konhaus
1969	Mrs. Carol H. Konhaus
1970	Mrs. Carol H. Konhaus
1971	Mrs. Carol H. Konhaus
1972	Mrs. Joseph C. Gribb
1973	*No Championship*
1974	Mrs. Earl L. Miller
1975	Mrs. Earl L. Miller
1976	Mrs. Earl L. Miller
1977	Mrs. Earl L. Miller
1978	Mrs. Earl L. Miller
1979	Mrs. Robert S. Fenton
1980	Mrs. Earl L. Miller
1981	Mrs. Drue S. Fenton
1982	Mrs. Earl L. Miller
1983	Mrs. Foster Q. Hopkins
1984	Mrs. Drue S. Fenton
1985	Mrs. Earl L. Miller
1986	Mrs. James T. Mardis
1987	Rusty Miller
1988	Carol Miller Dressel
1989	Rusty Miller
1990	Mrs. Gloria Basehore
1991	Mrs. Dianne Kollas

HUSBAND & WIFE CHAMPIONS

1960	Mr. & Mrs. Fred McDonell
1961	Mr. & Mrs. John Williamson
1962	Mr. & Mrs. Ed Parkinson
1963	Mr. & Mrs. Fred McDonell
1964	Mr. & Mrs. Leroy Clark
1965	Mr. & Mrs. Jack Murphy
1966	Mr. & Mrs. Earl Miller
1967	Mr. & Mrs. Jack Murphy
1968	Mr. & Mrs. Clark Stecher
1969	Mr. & Mrs. Earl Miller
1970	Dr. & Mrs. Frank Procopio
1971	Dr. & Mrs. Frank Procopio
1972	Mr. & Mrs. Robert Meck
1973	Mr. & Mrs. Robert Meck
1974	Mr. & Mrs. Earl Miller
1975	Mr. & Mrs. Foster Hopkins
1976	Mr. & Mrs. Charles Hoffman
1977	Mr. & Mrs. George Botts
1978	Mr. & Mrs. Charles Hoffman
1979	Mr. & Mrs. Foster Hopkins
1980	Mr. & Mrs. Louis Landino
1981	Mr. & Mrs. Robert Meck
1982	Mr. & Mrs. James Szoke
1983	Mr. & Mrs. Jack Blair

1984	Mr. & Mrs. Stephen Borowitz
1985	Mr. & Mrs. Robert Meck
1986	Mr. & Mrs. William Abbe
1987	Mr. & Mrs. Foster Hopkins
1988	Mr. & Mrs. Clay Taylor
1989	Mr. & Mrs. Walter Fry, Jr.
1990	Mr. & Mrs. Earl Miller
1991	Mr. & Mrs. Walter Fry, Jr.
1992	Mr. & Mrs. Robert Meck
1993	Mr. & Mrs. Walter Fry, Jr.
1994	Rita & George Patterson
1995	Caryn & Luke Rohrbaugh
1996	Irene & Harry Dissinger
1997	Rita & Harry Warren
1998	Caryn & Luke Rohrbaugh
1999	Martha & Al Heidenwolf
2000	Marri Lamoureaux & Dave Wrye
2001	Melissa & Andy Buzby
2002	Mary Elanor & Dick Patterson
2003	Carla & Dick Brokenshire
2004	Linda & Sal Alfano
2005	Linda & Sal Alfano
2006	Lisa & Ted Mowery
2007	Lisa & Ted Mowery
2008	Nancy & Jim Thomas

MEN'S MEMBER-GUEST CHAMPIONS

1964	John Johnson	M. Beldon
1965	R. Tye	B. Butler
1966	A. McKechnie	W. Shultz
1967	J. Cleveland	R. McEldowney
1968	*No Competition*	
1969	L. Landino	H. Johnson
1970	F. Wigfield III	D. Bruce
1971	J. Cleveland	D. Bruce
1972	C. Kitzmiller	D. King
1973	R. Fenton	J. Martz
1974	B. Husted	S. McKeon
1975	C. Leggett	T. Leggett
1976	W. Sutphen	W. Adams
1977	C. Delone	P. Delone
1978	J. Twigg	B. Myers
1979	W. McCall	P. Paturzo, Jr.
1980	F. Mosher	R. Davis
1981	David Dodd	Donald Dvorak
1982	Don Post	Dave Post
1983	Buddy Cummings	Edward Driscoll
1984	John Snoke	Howard Schake
1985	Robert Dietz	Denis Chagnon

1986	Hank Johnson	Paul Cercel
1987	Thomas Sullivan	Charles Nelo
1988	Ken Greider	John Malady
1989	Bill Dick	Charles Jensik
1990	Don Lund	Bill Keyte
1991	Carl Schleicher	Ed Ionni
1992	Jim Green, Jr.	Dave Lis
1993	Jay Cleveland, Jr.	Jim Fox
1994	Sal Alfano	Bob Beaudry
1995	Mark Reilly	Bob Reilly
1996	John Burleson	Charles Jensik
1997	Don Magnuski	Glen Montgomery
1998	John Burleson	Charles Jensik
1999	Marshall Davis	Gordon Banzhoff
2000	Jim Green, Jr.	Courtney Smyth
2001	Dennis Brenckle	Dennis Fingers
2002	Rick Scott	Steve Borowitz
2003	Ray Hoover	Steve Sninski
2004	Marty Jackson	Tony McIntyre
2005	Rob Strewig	Hap Campbell
2006	Don Sunderland	Mike Guimond
2007	Gary Poffenberger	Brad Boyer
2008	Jack Jurasits	Gary Frantz

MEN'S MEMBER-MEMBER CHAMPIONS

1988	Ed Kelly	Bill Schumacher
1989	Don Failor	Carl Schleicher
1990	Hugh Rozman	Dick Mauch
1991	Bill Slike	Tom Stone
1992	Fred Gettys	Ron Smith
1993	Foster Hopkins	Alex McKechnie
1994	George Dimoff	Bill McCall
1995	Steve Borowitz	Jim Tabor
1996	Charles Gutshall	Richard Murphy
1997	Ron Scott	Rick Scott
1998	Hank Seidel	Nelson Swarts
1999	Don Leggett	Harry Warren
2000	James Lozano	Rob Meier
2001	Rob Gothier	Marty Jackson
2002	Rob Gothier	Marty Jackson
2003	George Pote	Glen Ressler
2004	Hank Seidel	Nelson Swarts
2005	Sam Botte	Bob Kessler, Jr.
2006	Ron Scott	Rick Scott
2007	Bob Beaudry	Marty Pastuka
2008	Ron Scott	Rick Scott

MEN'S SENIOR GOLF CHAMPIONS

1998	E. James Tabor
1999	Bill Stasiulatis
2000	Hank Johnson
2001	Bill McCall
2002	George Dimoff
2003	Bill Stasiulatis
2004	Bill Stasiulatis
2005	Rick Scott
2006	Bill McCall
2007	R. Scott Christie
2008	R. Scott Christie

ED TABOR INVITATIONAL CHAMPIONS

1975	Pat McLaughlin	Scott Schwartz
1976	Rick Hrip	Charles Stringfellow
1977	Rick Hrip	Charles Stringfellow
1978	Rick Hrip	Charles Stringfellow
1979	Rick Hrip	Charles Stringfellow
1980	Joe Higgins	John Trach
1981	Stu Ingraham	Scott Stoner
1982	John Trach	Pete Gebhard
1983	Rick Hrip	Charles Stringfellow
1984	Rick Hrip	Charles Stringfellow
1985	Rick Hrip	Charles Stringfellow
1986	R. Scott Christie	Joe Faller
1987	Walter Jacobs	Dennis Woolf
1988	Michael Byrnes	William Bratina
1989	Randy Valk	Jeff Sunday
1990	John Trach	Warren Gittlen
1991	Jeff Sunday	Bob Olsen
1992	Jim Koury	Chris Slike
1993	R. Scott Christie	Joe Faller
1994	Chuck Tait	Bob Teufel
1995	Jim Koury	Chris Slike
1996	Dave Walker	Ed Short
1997	Rick Hrip	Charles Stringfellow
1998	R. Scott Christie	George Dimoff
1999	Roger Karsnitz	Rick Troutman
2000	John Trach	Charles Stringfellow
2001	William Smith	Charles Rahauser
2002	Scott Mayne	Jim Hughes
2003	Charles Stringfellow	Jeff Frazier
2004	Jeff Ernst	Ed Short
2005	Charles Stringfellow	Jeff Frazier
2006	Greg Lesher	Chris Gebhard
2007	Roger Karsnitz	Ryan Schneiter
2008	Roger Karsnitz	Ryan Schneiter

TENNIS PROS AT WEST SHORE COUNTRY CLUB

1974		Pat Harry
1975-76		Stan Bourne
1977	Andy Harrison	Mark Cooper
	provided by Washington Tennis Service	
1977		Pat Harry
1979-80		George Garland
1980-81		Sue Ruhl
1982		William Lantz
1983-84		Don Talbert
1985-86		Stratin (Chip) Sheaffer
1987-88		David Schall
1989-91		Mark Tyndall
1992		Pat Woolford
1994-95		Jake Ray
1996		John Weaver
1997-00		Kason Henery
2004-06		Kevin Scott
2007-09		Frank Petri

TENNIS CHAMPIONS

	MEN'S SINGLES	MEN'S DOUBLES
1974	Chuck Fromer	
1975	Jack Myers	
1976	Chuck Fromer	Chuck Fromer / Chris Fry
1977	Chuck Fromer	Chuck Sieck / Bob Spitzer
1978	Paul Matisse	
1980	Bob Hollaway	
1981	Earl Weaver	Earl Weaver / Jim Weaver
1982	Chuck Fromer	Chuck Fromer / Bill Forbrich
1983	Chuck Fromer	David Briel / Mike Baum
1984	Jack Myers	David Briel / Mike Baum
1985	Paul Matisse	Paul Matisse / Chuck Fromer
1986	Paul Matisse	Paul Matisse / Chuck Fromer
1987	Paul Matisse	
1989	Paul Matisse	Paul Matisse / Chuck Fromer
1991		Mervin Holland / John Purcell

1997	Jim Keys	Merv Holland / Jack Meyers
1998	Jim Keys	Jim Keys / Jim Robertson
1999	Ed Fetrow	Greg Aversa / Samir Srouji
2000	Jim Keys	
2001	Ed Fetrow	Ed Fetrow / John Noone
2002	Jim Keys	Jim Keys / Jim Robertson
2003	John Noone	Ed Fetrow / John Noone
2004	Ed Fetrow	Joe Dixon / Dave Sweet
2005	Peter Ballantine	Ed Fetrow / John Noone
2006	Alden Cunningham	Alden Cunningham / Jim Keys
2007		John Noone / Joe Navin

	WOMEN'S SINGLES	**WOMEN'S DOUBLES**
1974	Carol Beatty	Barbara Beatty / Carol Beatty
1975	Barbara Beatty	Barbara Beatty / Carolyn Setzer
1976	Barbara Beatty	Barbara Beatty / Carolyn Setzer
1976	Carolyn Setzer	Barbara Beatty / Carolyn Setzer
1977	Phyllis Mowery	Phyllis Mowery / Donna Saxon
		Barbara Beatty / Carolyn Setzer
1980	Marge Weaver	Lynn Freitas / Joan Costello
1981	Patt Schmidt	Joan Costello / Lynn Freitas
1982	Marge Weaver	Joan Costello / Lynn Freitas
1983	Marge Weaver	
1984	Ingrid Conner	Joan Costello / Lynn Freitas
1985	Phyllis Mowery	Patt Schmidt / Ingrid Conner

1986	Shirley Beane	Lynn Freitas / Joan Costello
1990	Shirley Beane	Joan Costello / Lynn Freitas
1991	Andrea Bromberg	Phyllis Mowery / Grace Robertson
2002	Carla Brokenshire	
2003	Diane Navin	Sandra Renninger / Grace Robertson
2004	Diane Navin	Kristi Arndt / Debra Stumpf
2005	Diane Navin	Kristi Arndt / Debra Stumpf
2006		Natalie Grubb / Sue Grammes

MIXED DOUBLES

1974	Carol Beatty / Chuck Fromer
1975	Barb Beatty / Chuck Fromer
1976	Donna Saxon / Merv Holland
1977	Chris Forbrick / Bill Forbrick
1980	Lynn Freitas / Andy Freitas
1981	Lynn Freitas / Andy Freitas
1982	Lynn Freitas / Andy Freitas
1983	Lynn Freitas / Andy Freitas
1984	Lynn Freitas / Andy Freitas
1985	Lynn Freitas / Andy Freitas
1986	Lynn Freitas / Andy Freitas
1989	Grace Robertson / Jim Robertson
1990	Lynn Freitas / Andy Freitas
2004	Diane Navin / Joe Navin

2009 Board of Governors   2009 Executive Staff

Fifty-year Members

NAME	JOINED		
Mr. Edward C. Michener	1938	Mr. John W. Gross, Jr.	1956
Mrs. Robert C. Shaw, Jr.	1938	Mr. J. William Royer	1956
Mrs. William H. Wood	1943	Mr. Lester G. Connor	1956
Mrs. John MacMurray	1945	Dr. Raymond C. Grandon	1957
Mrs. Max C. Hempt	1947	Mr. Richard E. Jordan	1957
Mrs. Martha R. Musselman	1947	Mrs. Kenneth E. Wolfe	1957
Mrs. Leon S. Shedlosky	1948	Mr. Harry W. Preis	1957
Dr. Joseph C. Gribb	1949	Mr. Howell C. Mette	1957
Mrs. Robert N. Striewig	1949	Mrs. G. W. Yamall	1957
Mrs. Charles E. Thomas, Sr.	1951	Mr. Foster Q. Hopkins	1957
Ms. Geraldine W. Shahian	1951	Dr. Frank Procopio	1957
Mr. James F. Scouler	1951	Mrs. Jane Zerby	1957
Mrs. Mason W. Denison	1953	Dr. Charles A. Delone	1958
Dr. Alex J. McKechnie, Jr.	1953	Dr. Herbert Jordan	1958
Mr. C. Ted Lick	1954	Mrs. Cleve J. Fredrickson	1958
Mr. James F. Penny, Jr.	1954	Mr. Robert G. Meck	1958
Ms. Elizabeth J. Maskel	1955	Sen. Harold F. Mowery, Jr.	1958
Dr. William F. Carr	1956	Mrs. Jane Zerby	1958

Past Presidents

1928	Franklin Davies	1971	John R. Dietz
1929	J. C. Arbegast	1972	Lester G. Conner
1930	C. A. Carl	1973	Reginald P. Seavey
1931	Christian L. Siebert	1974	Horace A. Johnson
1932	Harold C. Whitcomb	1975	William J. Healey
1933	Harold C. Whitcomb	1976	Vance L. Scout
1934	Herman F. Keihl	1977	George F. Patterson
1935	Leon D. Metzger	1978	E. L. "Jack" Gaughen
1936	Fred V. Rocky	1979	William T. Kirchhoff
1937	George N. Wade	1980	William F. Sutphen
1938	John A. Wickenhaver	1981	James L. Royer
1939	John B. Lee	1982	L. Robert Kessler
1940	George I. Fisher	1983	Kenneth E. Wolfe
1941	Charles W. Hull	1984	Frank A. Mosher
1942	T. M. Snedden	1985	Blair G. Husted
1943	Joseph R. Farrell	1986	Elmer R. Reichwald
1944	R. A. Eisiminger	1987	John A. Plesic
1944	Joseph A. Hayes	1988	H. Robert Lasday
1945	Howard B. White	1989	William A. Lake
1946	Elmer A. Groene	1990	Ronald H. Smith
1947	Harold B. Miller	1991	A. L. Marks, Jr.
1948	W. E. Young	1992	James E. Grandon, Jr.
1949	W. W. Sponsler	1993	Jay W. Cleveland
1950	Richard T. Tyner	1994	Richard E. Jordan II
1951	Robert H. Stewart	1995	Gomer L. Stephenson III
1952	John C. Kelly	1996	James A. Smeltzer
1953	F. W. Musselman	1997	Dale E. Blair
1954	Edward A. C. Bennett	1998	Lee C. Turner
1955	Karl L. Gatter	1999	John J. Bolger
1956	Charles N. Fritz	2000	J. Dixon Earley
1957	Lee C. Hinds	2001	Nelson A. Swarts
1958	Ray R. Ramsey	2002	Kenneth W. Fry
1959	L. Edward Sprague	2003	Brice D. Arndt
1960	W. Dixon Morrow	2004	Ralph S. Klinepeter, Jr.
1961	Elmer A. Groene	2005	Jeffrey H. Gribb
1962	William H. Wood	2006	William D. Greenlee
1963	William M. Colestock, Jr.	2007	Thomas G. Holtzman
1964	Royal L. Cleveland	2008	Henry Line
1965	Raymond E. Bowman		
1966	Richard E. Jordan		
1967	Edward C. Michener		
1968	Robert W. Helms		
1969	John A. Johnson		
1970	James K. Thomas